Ways Out

Ways Out

The Book of Changes for Peace

EDITED BY
Gene Knudsen-Hoffman

A JIM COOK EDITION

JOHN DANIEL & COMPANY · SANTA BARBARA · 1988

Wendell Berry: "Plant Sequoias" first appeared in *Collected Poems, 1957-1982*, North Point Press (Berkeley, CA), 1985.

Thich Nhat Hanh: "Can You Be More Than American?" "Reconciliation, Not Victory," and "Can You Write a Love Letter to Your Congressperson?" all first appeared in *Being Peace*, Parallex Press (Berkeley, CA).

David Hoffman: "Green Zones" is excerpted from "Evolutionary Blues." Reprinted with the author's permission.

Mary Evelyn Jegen, M.D.: "Benevolent Glancing" first appeared in *Sisters Today*, 58:8, April 1987.

Frances Kendell and Jean Louw: "South Africa: The Decentralist Alternative" first appeared in *After Apartheid: The Solution for South Africa*, by ICS Press (San Francisco).

Gene Keyes: "Force Without Firepower" first appeared in *Co-Evolution Quarterly No. 34*, Summer 1982 (pgs. 4-25).

Mark Satin: "Macy: A Movement That Works," ©New Options, August 27, 1984 (P.O. Box 19324, Washington, DC 20036). "Robertson: From Jobs to Ownwork," ©New Options, April 28, 1986. "Self Reliance Goes Mainstream," ©New Options, October 21, 1985.

Mark Shepard: "Justice That Unites," "Shanti Sena: India's Peace Brigade," and "Let The Forest Rise" all first appeared in *Gandhi Today: The Story of Mahatma Gandhi's Successors*, Seven Locks Press (Cabin John, MD), 1987.

Kurt Vonnegut: "War Preparers Anonymous" first appeared in *The Nation*, The Nation Co., Inc., Dec. 31, 1983.

LIBRARY OF CONGRESS CATALOGING IN PUBLICATION DATA
Ways out: the book of changes for peace / Gene Knudsen-Hoffman, editor.
    ISBN 0-936784-51-2 (pbk.) : $9.95
    1. Peace. 2. Violence I. Knudsen-Hoffman, 1919-
JX1963.W325 1988
327.1'72—dc 19   87-35219 CIP

Book design and typography by Jim Cook, Santa Barbara, California.

Published by John Daniel & Company, Post Office Box 21922, Santa Barbara, California 93121.

To my teachers . . .

- My mother, who never closed any doors to her heart.
- My father, who taught me to seek my own truths.
- My former husband, Hallock Hoffman, who taught me I was a vessel of truth.
- Stephen Levine, who taught me to keep my heart open in hell.
- Ram Dass, who taught me that acting from anger breeds anger, not peace.
- My Quakers, who taught me it is more important to love the good than to hate the evil.
- Thich Nhat Hanh, who taught me I must seek to *be* peace.
- Mother Teresa, who taught me that everyone—even the rapist, the rich, and the warmaker—"is Christ," sometimes "in distressing disguise."
- Nieves, who taught me if someone wounded me I should "Bless them and let them go."
- Armando Quiros, who taught me those "Bright shinings of truth" which sometimes enter my consciousness can be called "God."
- My children, who taught me how deeply I can wound.
- My twelve step people, who taught me all wounds can be healed.

CONTENTS

Regional Ways Out

Global Ways Out

x

Gene Knudsen-Hoffman:

INTRODUCTION

Long ago I learned that the first step to nonviolence is saying a loud, strong NO. It may be the last step, too. But what comes in between? That's today's question.

I've been watching media for a long time. They make available many solutions for problems that assail us. Most of these solutions are violent. I have seen few spokespersons for nonviolent alternatives on radio or TV or in the press. I began to wonder why. It occurred to me that perhaps none of us who claim to be nonviolent had thought of any alternatives. I wondered if perhaps we were too busy trying to understand nonviolence ourselves, and in the meantime all we knew to do was say *no*.

I thought of England's "shadow government." Members of the loyal opposition, those out of power, meet to deliberate on critical issues facing their government and make their proposals known to the public, so that people have an opportunity to consider alternatives and make informed choices.

And I wondered: What if we citizens decided that the responsibilities of citizenship demanded new efforts from us? What if *we* must create new policy and present it to the public if we hope to change our government's actions? In my view, it's time we developed alternatives to our government's violent policies and offered them to our representatives and to the media. In this way, we could educate people, and our government, to new views on old problems.

In January 1987, I sent letters to about three hundred people, inviting each to submit a brief essay, a concise statement of an idea for a nonviolent alternative to any national or international problem that concerned them. "What is your critical issue?" I asked. "What aspect of our world's violence bothers you most? And what ideas have you to turn that situation around? Feel free to write on any problem, domestic or international: joblessness, homelessness, monopolies, our economy, militarism, crime, terrorism, hostages, Latin America, the Middle East...." There was only one guideline set for them: their proposal had to reduce fear. I believe that any initiative, anywhere, from the summit to the city council, which reduces fear can lead toward a world without war. I also set one limitation: their ideas had to be presented in five hundred words or less. Each could, however, send in as many separate essays as he or she had to offer.

I also asked each person to recommend others who might contribute to the book. Soon I had a huge mailing list of potential contributors. I wrote to them all. Their solutions came pouring in. The cooperation from editors and authors was amazing, and the depth and richness of the ideas presented was astonishing. By the end of a year, I had hundreds of articles to choose among.

Making the final selection for this book was both a great pleasure and a very difficult task. There was a wealth of material from which to choose, and we had room for only one bookful. In the long run, I relied on the criteria set forth in my initial invitation to participate in the book: I have chosen articles that stress the reduction of fear; articles that offer something fresh and innovative (or at least present a new way of looking at a solution that I hadn't come across before); and, especially, articles that offer positive, constructive, reconciling solutions. (For the purpose of this book I have used these definitions of reconcilitation: to bring together those who have been separated or set apart; to bring back into community those who have been exiled; and Thich Nhat Hanh's definition, to understand both sides.) This book is not a collection of protests and *no*'s. It is a collection of productive ideas for building a world that is to be, not for destroying the world that is. The book is divided into three sections—personal, regional, and global—since these areas seem to be the focus of the solutions offered, although the theories and attitudes behind the solutions often overlap and work for all three categories.

I might add that I don't agree wholeheartedly with every idea included here; but each idea presented is worth thinking about, and in many cases worth acting on. The other thing to say, of course, is that the book is only a beginning, offered to get us started in the right direction, and to show how much creativity for peace there is in all of us. The ways out of our violent problems are in place in people's hearts and minds. Now we need to develop the energy and will to implement these ideas and create more.

Many people have my gratitude for their help in creating this book. First, of course, I thank each and all the contributors for their ideas and for indulging me in my need to fit their copy to the restraints of this collection. And the many others who helped turn mountains of paperwork into a book, especially book designer and editorial cheerleader Jim Cook, for wonderful hours of productive brainstorming.

Wendell Berry:

PLANT SEQUOIAS

... So, friend, every day do something
that won't compute. Love the Lord.
Love the world. Work for nothing.
Take all that you have and be poor.
Love someone who does not deserve it.
Denounce the government and embrace
the flag. Hope to live in that free
Republic for which it stands.
Give your approval to all you cannot
understand. Praise ignorance, for what man
has not encountered he has not destroyed.
Ask the questions that have no answers.
Invest in the millennium. Plant sequoias.
Say that your main crop is the forest
that you did not plant,
that you will not live to harvest.
Say that the leaves are harvested
when they have rotted into the mold.
Call that profit. Prophesy such returns.
Put your faith in the two inches of humus
that will build under the trees every thousand years.
Listen to carrion—put your ear
close, and hear the faint chattering
of the songs that are to come.
Expect the end of the world. Laugh.
Laughter is immeasurable. Be joyful
though you have considered all the facts.
... Go with your love to the fields.

Lie easy in the shade. rest your head
in her lap. Swear allegiance
to what is highest in your thoughts.
As soon as the generals and the politicos
can predict the motions of your mind,
lose it. Leave it as a sign
to mark the false trail, the way
you didn't go. Be like the fox
who makes more tracks than necessary,
some in the wrong direction.
Practice resurrection.

From MANIFESTO:
The Mad Farmer Liberation Front

Personal Ways Out

Toby Steffian:

TEACHING NONVIOLENT POWER TO CHILDREN

When my daughter was eight years old, I had to make an anti-nuclear talk to a small group, and couldn't afford a sitter for her. I didn't think she should come to the meeting and hear about nuclear destruction. My solution then, was to bring her along, but also to tell her that we would take some toys in the car so she could play in the room next to the meeting room.

When we arrived, I asked her to bring in the toys. She refused, saying she would be uncomfortable alone in a room in this strange building. I accepted her refusal, took her to the meeting, and omitted the material on nuclear destruction. She won.

Afterward, I told her that what she had done in refusing to take in the toys was nonviolent action—in this case, conscientious disobedience. I told her that this was good, and I hoped she would do it again. She was performing the concept of nonviolent noncooperation.

Occasionally, my daughter has disobeyed me again, and each

time I have considered her claim of justice and capitulated if I agreed with it, or avoided giving in to her if I could.

Each time I have made sure that she understood that she was doing nonviolent action.

It is good for the learning of nonviolence to begin in childhood; if the teaching is to be consistent, nonviolence must be usable against us parents and teachers. To teach the civil disobedience part of nonviolence, we reinforce the principle of nonviolence behind the natural disobedience children practice with us. Children practice nonviolence by crying, which can make powerful parents capitulate. Crying is an example of nonviolent protest. Later, children become nonviolent activists through adolescent rebellion.

What sort of person has this child, whose parent has urged her to disobey him, turned out to be? Is she selfish? Her friends say that she is not; justice not greed wins for her. Is she undisciplined? Her teachers say she is one of the most disciplined children in school. After all, she doesn't have the displaced anger that can come from having no tools to get her way when she believes, in conscience, that she should have it. Does she disobey others besides me? Yes, occasionally. Is my authority reduced with her? I think it is increased. I believe that her character has improved as a result of my encouraging her to disobey.

Another result is that my daughter's natural ability to say "no" has been strengthened, which should be useful when she is old enough to face the possibility of sexual abuse from dates. She knows she can say "no" to her father without losing his love so she should be more able to say "no" to dates than many females are in cases where saying "no" can prevent abuse. One effect of her saying "no" to me has been for me to remove my arm from her shoulder when she has not wanted it there. That action is an example of nonviolent intervention, which, with noncooperation and protest described above, add up to an inclusive set of three forms of nonviolent action. She has had reflective practice in them all.

Sometimes I use nonviolence against my daughter and thus

become a model. For example, when she was very young, I used to perform sit-down strikes against her, refusing to play with her or do anything else until she behaved. The tactic also gave me time to think what else I could do when I was stumped.

The paradox is that by encouraging disobedience in conscience in our children, as well as by encouraging obedience, we may be able to raise more powerful, obedient, unresentful, and unselfish children. Perhaps one reason that this encouragement is so rare is that when children have strong skills in nonviolence, parents have to eat crow more often and kids win against their parents more often. But they should.

Carol S. Wolman-Clapsadle, M.D.:

DIVORCE

Sixty percent of American marriages now end in divorce. Over half of those who unite in love then give up on the power of love to solve problems. Marriage used to be a sacrament, a lifelong commitment for better or worse. The high divorce rates implies that many no longer believe in a God of love who helps men and women grow together through the turmoil of family life. Many no longer honor their deepest life commitment, becoming numbed and cynical.

Children of divorcing parents experience a mini nuclear war, with total destruction of their nuclear family and home. Afterward they are shellshocked, torn in two. They have great difficulty believing in a normal family life, and lose faith that they can form an enduring family when adult.

As a woman, with a sometimes stormy marriage and two small children, I have sadly learned that divorce is not only condoned, it is encouraged. When we have turned to friends and professionals for help, my husband is usually labelled the "bad guy" and I am encouraged to leave him. In the Christian community we have found support for our determination to work out our problems and mature through this struggle, as people have always done—until recently.

It is no accident that the divorce rate skyrocketed after the invention of nuclear weapons. The threat to survival and the future leads to psychic numbing, which, in turn, destroys human bonding.

Conversely, when a person divorces a mate, s/he is rejecting his/her natural partner for working to reverse the arms race, save the environment, and safeguard the future. For it is the love spouses have for each other and for their children that is the wellspring of life, and which provides the psychic energy to protect them and to push society to do what it should. Without strong family units committed to the future, there is little hope for positive change.

I therefore encourage all people concerned with survival to examine their own lives and look at their commitment to family. Acknowledge their mistakes, grieve over their losses, and resolve to make their current marital partner their lifelong one. Let this be the person with whom they build a strong family so that the children may feel secure; the person with whom they learn to solve conflicts as the nations must learn to solve theirs; the person with whom they work for peace on the planet. I believe that God can forgive our mistakes, heal our weaknesses, and fill us with the love we need to do all this.

Gene Knudsen-Hoffman:

REFLECTIONS ON ABORTION

I've been thinking about abortion so I could discover what I think about abortion. I've found all the reasons for it so logical, so persuasive, so right: no more unwanted children; children should not live in emotional, physical, or spiritual squalor; women should have rights over their own bodies.

I agree with all of the above and probably more—and yet, and yet—there's a "stop" in me.

"Abortion," comes the message, "is not turning toward fuller life; it's turning toward diminution, toward death." How does it differ from any other killing?

I know that abortion is frequently the "lesser evil"; it may be a necessity today because we have not found a more life-affirming way to deal with our sexuality and its consequences.

So, if no abortions—what do we do about couplings which result in unwanted pregnancies?

The only way I see clear at present is to change our individual attitudes. What if we celebrated parenthood in whatever form it took? What if we recognized the holiness of life however it emerges? What if our society considered parenthood an honor, a gift, and we knew the newborn came "with angels trailing"? What if we knew each fetus carried a seed which could flower into a new bright message?

And then, if we were really hospitable to the wonder of children, might not our sexuality have fresh meaning? It might cease being a blind burrowing for satisfaction, the endless pursuit of elusive ecstasy, an anodyne to pain, a sometime pleasurable substitute for television, a tool of power, or a frantic distraction from reality.

Perhaps if we cherished our sexuality more, it might bless us, instead of taunting us with insatiable hunger.

Then this marvelous, mysterious force that can impregnate us with the child of flesh or spirit might be restored to its sacred place. And then—there might be more joy in our world, for we could welcome with more attention, more delight, these tiny guests to our lives.

Genie Durland:

ON ABORTION: ANOTHER OPTION

We have a friend—a young mother of two in training to be a midwife—who, as a Christian pacifist, is deeply opposed to abortion. However, instead of preaching against abortion to women in trouble or demonstrating at abortion clinics, she decided to try in her small way to provide an alternative. She opened her home to these women as a refuge. In her midwifery work, when she came upon a woman contemplating abortion because of financial desperation, aloneness, or rejection by parents and/or the father of the child, she offered the woman a home with her. She provided food, shelter, companionship, and support during the pregnancy and, in some cases, beyond. She struggled to help the women in her care to find the appropriate options for themselves and their babies after leaving her home.

6

Mary Porter-Chase:

RECONCILIATION AMONG HEALING TECHNIQUES?

Health care in the United States is provided primarily by allopathic (conventional) medicine. Although it offers the best crisis care in the world and has managed to control and in some cases eliminate certain diseases, allopathy has a violent nature to it as well. It incorporates skills, technologies, and drugs whose very language suggests violence and alienation: attack and conquer, seek and destroy, killing germs, removing parts, transplanting organs, attacking and eliminating viruses and foreign bodies that invade the body, covering up pain, and conquering disease.

There are, however, rich and diverse alternatives to this allopathic system—nonviolent healing resources that work to naturally strengthen the immune system, balance and free energy, align our physical structure, soften our angers, tonify our organs, lighten our depressions, and lift our spirits. Without harmful side-effects or the creation of a new illness, and without weakening the body's ability to heal itself.

If I were in an influential position in our society, I would bring into balance and harmony the healing techniques and approaches of all legitimate and competent health-care modes.

In this way I feel people would be able, many times in their lives, to engage in nonviolent healing and thus create a more trusting, gentle, peaceful, and intimate relationship with their bodies.

Corporate medicine includes allopathic medine, insurance and governmental agencies, mass media and pharmaceutical companies—all of which work together in such ways that they support, "feed," and strengthen each other, and thus weaken healing modalities other than the mainstream allopathic system. I would monitor and regulate this acitivity to prevent such symbiotic relationships that were not in the best interest of the patients as consumers.

I would have a fully conscious national health-care plan so that all people would have free and easy access to the best medical care of their choice.

I would define primary health-care practitioners to include Native American healers, acupuncturists, homeopaths, chiropractors, naturopaths, and herbologists, as well as M.D.s.

Qualified practioners of non-allopathic modalities would not be called "alternative." They would be allowed to practice side-by-side with M.D.s as primary health-care professionals.

All hospitals would be required to have toxic-free zones in separate wings or floors where only whole foods and quality water would be fed to patients. Any health practioners using toxic-free treatments would be welcome to have their patients in these zones.

I would help all primary health-care professionals understand and value each other's philosophies and techniques.

I would require that all primary health-care professionals be exposed to spiritual experiences that connect them to their inner light and wisdom. My system would provide them with time and opportunities to integrate their spiritual experiences into their personal lives and their work.

I would create centers where people could go to acquaint themselves with all forms of healing in an unbiased, professional, and thorough way. People then would be able to select the system that would best keep them well or treat their particular condition.

Once people are informed and have a way to finance their health care, they will more frequently select less violent approaches to much of their healing.

8

Albert V. Baez:

EDUCATION: THE FOUR C's

W e hear a great deal these days about the need for the United States to regain its competitive edge in industry. There is an even greater need for learning how to cooperate with people. We tout the value of competition in education, but as a teacher for many years I wished I could harness the incentive of cooperation instead of the insane competition for grades.

A bright student could achieve two objectives at once by being *helpful* to a slower student. He could improve his own communication skills at the same time that he was helping the slower student understand.

We must promote an education that stresses the four C's: curiosity, creativity, competence, and compassion. Weisskopf has noted the complementarity between *curiosity* and *compassion* which underlies our humanity.

I was heartened to see a physicist express such thoughts. It prompted me to realize the complementarity between *competence* and *compassion*: competence without compassion is inhuman, while compassion without competence is ineffectual. This duality has recently been expressed by another physicist, Freeman Dyson: "Technology without morality is barbarous; morality without technology is impotent."

The most important of the four C's is compassion. It is the motivating force behind *respect* and *affection* for living things—plants, animals, people, and yes, the earth. It provides the ethical basis for a fifth C—conservation.

Einstein has written: "Our task must be to free ourselves from this prison [of considering ourselves separate from nature] by widening our circle of compassion to embrace all living creatures and the whole of nature in its beauty." Compassion is incompatible with violence.

"Spirit" Donna Bradley:

EDUCATION CAN BE
A HEALING PLACE

Celebrations is a special home for very special children. My husband and I are a family that adopts and cares for children who have been severely battered, sexually abused, or neglected. We currently have fifteen full-time children and seven who go between us and their parents. Almost all have come from institutional settings and have labels such as autistic, psychotic, multiple personality, suicidal, or retarded. We don't let these labels allow us to distance ourselves from these kids. There is some of them in each of us, and all human beings live and grow and heal in the same light.

From first morning hugs ("How did you sleep?") until evening's last kiss on the eyelids ("Remember to talk back in your dreams"), education is an every-moment process. How to take out the garbage, internal as well as external, becomes a fine art which all family members applaud when executed with grace.

Five days a week, school starts after breakfast when we gather to plan our day. We talk about how people are feeling, and what challenges are already apparent in the day's schedule. For children who have experienced little control over their own

10

lives, it is especially important not to feel a victim of the day. We consciously work into the conversation that people are loved and valued for just being themselves rather than for their productivity.

Ten-year-old David, who had played the part of his mother's husband since he was five, finds it almost impossible to believe that we will love him even if he needs not to act responsibly on a certain day.

Everyone volunteers for chores, knowing that they have the choice, with absolutely no guilt, to go to a quiet place and do what we call "internal cleanup." (We devised this after finding eight-year-old Manju, who was raised in India and had never bonded to anyone, hiding in the garbage can every morning just at clean-up time.) All of us go off to our jobs, knowing there is a definite end to the work time, since we will be gathering again in less than an hour for what the kids call "real" school. Having a definite closure to chores is important for children whose love (food, shelter, safety) has literally been taken away as punishment for work "poorly" done.

Real school has an academic focus three days each week. The most difficult task for the teachers is to create an atmosphere of success and pride for children who consider themselves "give-aways." Many of our children come from such abusive homes that school was considered the only safe haven.

Twice a week is experiential school. For example, last Tuesday was devoted to wolves. We all read about wolves, listened to recordings of wolves howling, howled ourselves, drew pictures, and wrote stories and poems. Fred, who is eleven going on five due to stress and malnutrition, stopped talking at the age of eight when he refused to testify against his father's torture and sexual abuse. Fred still doesn't speak very well, but he sure can howl. This week we recorded a discussion about the definition of love in honor of St. Valentine's day. Did the father who battered and raped Robyn really love her? We think so. Can we really love a child who comes to us so filled with self-hate that she ritualistically abuses herself? We know so.

Afternoons are for individual time with specific children.

Whether encouraging one to express some old hurt by helping to beat up a teddy bear, or admiring a teenager's art work, the message gets across: I cherish you as a special person who has unique gifts to offer the family, both ours and the world's.

The most significant part of our school happens around nine o'clock at night. We call it Sabbath, which means "to listen to, or return to, one's heart." Our Sabbath grew from an attempt to find something like Quaker meetings that would work for kids who have experienced something very traumatic or terrifying. We often begin Sabbath by explaining to the children that the most important thing we can teach them is how to get to real stillness. We light a candle and ask for stillness in body, mind, and heart. We break silence with a blessing song. Then each of us speaks of our day. For Sabbath to work, there must be immunity from censure or judgment, yet room for dialogue.

Angela must be encouraged to tell us that she stole from the grocery store, knowing that we will respond with ways to make amends, rather than punishment. Ananda must feel safe enough to speak of the connection she is making between the rapes that happened consistently at the ages of two, three, and four, and the spasticity in her body now at age ten. Each night we hold another layer of pain up to the healing light, and each night we feel better. There is no topic that is inappropriate and we don't feel depressed when we have a way to let go of the hurt and yet keep the love.

When all feel full, we sing "Family Sleeping Lord, Kumbaya (Come by Here)," and blow the candle out as a commitment to taking the light inside—eager for another day of loving, arguing, growing, and learning, knowing that everything these kids do is an attempt to get back to God.

12

Mary E. Clark:

NO MORE COMPETITION, PLEASE!

Competition, so highly touted in American society as basic to progress and to efficiency, we worship at our peril. We ignore that competition creates secrecy and suspicion, and that whenever there's a winner there's a loser. Competition, far from being healthy for a society, alienates us from one another. It destroys the very thing that matters *most* to human beings everywhere—a sense of belonging, of being wanted. And when a society does not provide that bondedness internally, it needs to create external "enemies" to hold its people together. Such a society becomes not only belligerent internationally, it tends to create violence within.

If one takes life seriously (as indeed we must), then there can be no such thing as friendly competition. There is a great deal of hypocrisy, for example, in teaching children sportsmanship by insisting they give three cheers for the other side after a football game. That kind of sportsmanship is just a way of legitimizing a desire for conquest and superiority. Likewise, supporting friendly economic competition is only a way to legitimize exploitation of workers in Third World nations and to defeat competitors at home. By glorifying competition, we ensure violence.

Cooperation, sharing, and reciprocal caring are what human nature is basically all about. Only when these aspects of life are *denied* do violence, greed, and exploitation emerge as cultural norms. Switching to nonviolence, then, means socially *unlearning* today's norms of competitive hierarchies, and teaching the young how to be truly cooperative and caring. This would mean eliminating competitive games; it would mean rethinking how we evaluate children's progress in schools; and ultimately it would mean constructing an economy where decision-making was *not* profit-motivated.

Non-competitive living is not at all boring. A Girl Scout camp I attended as a child had no competitive events whatsoever, yet we did not miss them. (It was only forty years later that I even realized there had been no competition.) We did things together. We all learned the same songs and sang them while hiking or waiting in line for dinner. We shared chores together, and these were rotated each day. We sketched and made crafts, folk-danced, put on plays and puppet shows, swam, did something called "pioneering," and sang around campfires. And it all was the most wonderful fun anyone can imagine. Moreover, it was as much fun for the adult counselors as for the children.

Noncompetition in schools will perhaps be harder to achieve. Yet one recent experiment I have tried at a university suggests it could work well. In a survey course about ethics and global issues, students are given twenty-five questions prior to the final so they can come up with soundly argued answers. Since the course stresses democracy and cooperation, we encourage them to study together, *and they do*. The first time I saw eight almost identical answers to a question it threw me. Collusion! But no. The students were— for the first time in their lives, too—doing what we were teaching them about: sharing their best ideas with each other. What is *wrong* with that? (In Japan, by the way, classes are promoted *en masse*, which provides powerful motivation for the "bright" students to assist the "slow" ones.)

Finally, cooperative economics would be community-based. Numerous experiments already exist in co-op movements and worker-owned and administered communities such as at Mondragon, Spain. And the tenets of the Green Party movement offer grassroots means for generating non-competitive political economies as well. Cooperation really is entirely feasible, after all.

Richard W. Fogg:

THE BRAIN DRAIN

Some localities are concerned about the brain drain from the community—particularly to the defense industry. Were they to build a series of scientific laboratories forbidden to do defense work, they could attract the highest scientific talent and upgrade the local industry and other institutions in the process.

Consider the situation of scientists completing a doctorate. They have dreamed of pursuing truth where it leads, and often all they can find are jobs in the defense industry. Many of these people don't want to contribute to the arms race, but their only alternative may then be to leave science. Half the scientists and engineers in this country are in defense work.

Thus, we need labs that allow freedoms in research unrelated to war.

In these labs, discoveries which lead to profitable inventions would bring the discoverer a bonus and a percent of profits— higher than is typical in industry today. The remainder of the profits from the inventions then would be plowed back into the lab.

There would be considerable freedom of work for the scientists, as in the Bell Labs, in the faith that this freedom would lead to profit. The labs would build and market their own inventions so as to reap the profits from their discoveries.

Quite probably, the brightest graduates in science in the U.S. would flock to such a lab to work; they would inevitably make discoveries that would be profitable, and therefore risk-capital could be found to build the labs.

Local businesses would have the opportunity to submit their scientific problems to the labs. That perk would attract new businesses.

Jim Forest:

FEELING SAFE

A woman in our community was walking home after midnight on an otherwise empty street in East Harlem. For some minutes she was aware of a man walking behind her, getting closer and closer. She was terrified and had no idea what to do—everything was closed, every door locked. Then she took what she called a "crazy gamble." She turned around, walked up to the man, and asked him if he could tell her where a certain subway stop was located. He looked confused, but told her.

Then she asked, "Please, would you walk me there? I'm afraid to be walking the streets by myself at night." He looked amazed, but agreed. He went with her as far as the subway entrance and then, with obvious embarrassment, said goodnight.

In one section of Philadelphia, local peace people set up a neighborhood solidarity program. One of the things they did was to hand out police whistles. Every woman had one in her purse and, if she felt threatened in any way, could take it out and blow it. By itself, a police whistle makes a lot of noise and is a powerful defense. But in this neighborhood, whoever heard someone blowing a whistle understood that they should join in. Within moments one whistle would be joined by many others. The woman—and the assailant—knew she wasn't alone.

16

Joanne Sheehan, a member of the Catholic Worker community in New York, always had a three-item "rape-prevention kit" in her bag. One was a police whistle she had bought for fifty cents. She also had an Alka Seltzer tablet—if needed, she could make herself foam at the mouth, "a definite turn-off for would-be rapists." Finally, she had a small light bulb, the size used in refrigerators. This was her lunatic defense. "I think people would avoid a woman who has a light bulb in her mouth," she said. "That light bulb in my bag makes me feel safe on the streets."

"Feeling safe." It isn't easy to feel safe and the truth is that we aren't safe. Life has never been safe, not in other centuries, not even in monasteries or on mountain tops. But it is much less safe in crowded cities, and still more dangerous in countries where deadly weapons are easily obtained and a lot of people are walking time bombs. But there are ways in which we can live more gracefully with insecurity. One doesn't have to live in constant dread. There are ways to empower ourselves. The ways don't come with guarantees, but they do give us the chance to take some constructive initiatives, to reach out, to surprise both ourselves and our opponents, and to humanize situations which otherwise might end tragically.

Judy Ellison:

THE GIFT OF TERROR

It seems important that we identify terror in our own hearts and relate to it personally. My own story of being forced to confront terrorism includes two incidents of the past year in Africa.

Early one Sunday morning a young Botswana man came to my front door and banged on it. "I need money, Ma, please give me money. I am hungry. I want some bread." I refused the young man money. He refused to leave. In his limited English he finally hit on the phrase, "What's it to you, Madam?"

I hate being called madam. I was angry at having my own resources questioned. In shame and desperation I handed over some *pula* notes. I was shaking. How did someone so crazed-looking get to my front door without my permission? I could not tell if he was high on drugs or just down and out. But clearly he was desperate and that scared me.

Another terror incident was the recent 2 A.M. raid on Gaborone by the South African defense forces. The raid was truly terrifying—every grenade, shot, explosion in ten locations in the city could be heard by me cowering in bed. Over loudspeakers I could hear the words of the invading terrorist troops as they ordered people out before blowing them away.

Not long after these incidents I found myself at a U.S. Embassy security briefing where the question in the hearts of all of us in the audience was what to do in case of a full invasion. Would we be evacuated in time (never mind in time for what)? The U.S. security official refused to address the terrorist raid and euphemistically told us that basic security included lighting our properties well, having several dogs (to ward off strangers like my young man), and hiring day and night security guards. I have joined the ranks of those expatriate Americans with security guards around the clock.

I confess to extreme ambivalence in participating in an official policy that seeks to remove the scare, the terror, from the hearts of Americans abroad by distancing us from the cares and concerns of our community. Here in Botswana, the state of drought and the proximity to South Africa engender *similar emotions* in both the well-off expatriate and the drought-stricken African. It is our *commonality* if we dare to let it be.

I suspect that in the U.S. we do a similar thing. We try to cover up terror with briefings, donations, laws, congressional hearings, and our global conscience and human rights image.

So under the carpet are swept battered women, abused children, starving peoples, homeless nations, all of whose first need is for someone who recognizes that their situation is terrifying and who is willing to sit with them in exactly that feeling state.

I have now begun to live with remembering where terror comes from—that sense of separateness—and what it leads us to do. I know this is not enough. But the gift that has come into my life in this last year is an experience of terror so great I know I must let it lead me to something new.

Alan R. Drengson:

AIKIDO: THE MARTIAL ART OF RECONCILIATION

Violence takes many forms in modern technological societies... Technology increases the magnitude of violence, although violence has its roots in more ancient habits of mind. Even if individual persons cannot immediately change the social structures that perpetuate violence, they can set their own lives straight. The evolutionary direction of change involves expanding our capacity to take responsibility for ourselves and to care for others.

How do we end long habits of violence? Is there a practice by means of which we can correct ourselves and heal our relationships?

Aikido is a martial art which emphasizes self discipline, courage, and endurance. It cultivates concentration and develops physical and spiritual strength. However it stresses non-fighting. It teaches one not to oppose force with force, or to answer violence in kind. It inculcates respect for others. Its practice helps one to root out the sources of violence in one's own mind. It teaches one to harmonize with a would-be opponent, not only in physical movement, but in spirit. Instead of creating contestants, Aikido teaches us to create friendships.

Founded in this century by Professor Morihei Uyeshiba (1883-1969), Aikido is often called the non-fighting martial art of harmony. Emphasis is on purifying one's mind of the seeds of conflict. It is based on a practical philosophy of mutual respect and interpersonal harmony: "Winning means winning over the mind of discord in yourself." (Uyeshiba).

The word *Aikido* reflects the basic philosophy of nonviolence that is at its heart; it means: "The way of harmonizing with the universal energy (or spirit) of the universe." Fighting arises from the desire to defend or extend one's ego-self (nation-self) boundaries. Instead of opposing an "opponent," Master Uyeshiba taught a *budo* (martial way) which harmonizes with others in spirit and in movement.

"The secret of Aikido is to harmonize ourselves with the movement of the universe and bring ourselves into accord with the universe itself." (Uyeshiba) To turn the spirit of reconciliation outward, after it has freed the self of the urge to fight, is to contribute to solving the basic problems of conflict and violence, for the harmony of love is at the heart of such action. Harmony can spread through our society just as readily as discord and violence, and it has far greater power for resolving our problems, which dominance and violence created in the first place.

Aikido helps one to realize with increasing depth the endless possibilities for constructive and creative interpersonal actions which benefit all of one's relationships. The energies it mobilizes not only unify the self, they also contribute to a growing sense that we can create peaceful communities reconciled with other communities and with nature.

The design and creation of new, nonviolent policies, institutions, and technologies requires that the designers be reconciled within themselves, with their communities, and with nature, for then the designs and practices would have protection of

20

ourselves, others, and nature built into them. Ultimately, to protect the environment and humankind, we must all follow a path of reconciliation.

Markley Morris:

NONVIOLENT SELF-DEFENSE

Why limit nonviolence to demonstrations? If nonviolence has power, surely this power is valid consistently and applies to any face-to-face conflict.

I experimented with nonviolent self defense when, as the result of a sit-in, I was serving a five-day sentence at antiquated, overcrowded San Francisco County Prison Two. My tier had about fifty one-man cells surrounding a wide hallway. During the day two prisoners were locked in each tiny cell. At night half of us—including me—were bedded down on filthy mattresses in the middle of the hallway.

Bobby, a young black trustee, clearly the most powerful prisoner on the tier, was my would-be rapist. To my surprise he had the pull to arrange with guards to have me transferred to his cell.

Probably the chief difference between my experience and most prison rapes is that I got to know my attacker in advance, a great advantage when it came to nonviolent defense.

Bobby was a fascinating man. He was in his late twenties and wore his hair in a sculptured pompadour. Like many prisoners, Bobby was highly intelligent but so poorly educated he could scarcely write his name. He agreed he'd probably spend half his life behind bars, but said he'd live high the rest of the time. He was cruel and arrogant, a bully at the top of the prison pecking order. He showed me a homemade stiletto, filed down from a dinner knife to a mean-looking blade. Possessing such a weapon in prison is a felony, so I was impressed.

From the first, Bobby made sexual advances and threats. The night before my release he got serious. He risked losing his "good time" by having another prisoner take his place in his cell so he could sleep out in the hallway. He put his mattress beside mine and told me he was going to fuck me. I could see I was going to have some night.

The prisoners around us knew what Bobby was up to and obligingly dropped off to sleep immediately. Bobby held the stiletto against my throat. I felt it pressing on my Adam's apple, and was so frightened I didn't dare swallow, but I kept talking. Bobby ordered me to take off my clothes. I said no, looked him in the eye, and braced myself for the cut. He kept ordering me and I kept talking, trying to sound calm.

Finally he said he was going to undress me. I struggled to keep him from rolling me over on my belly. He tore at my pants hard enough to pop off the buttons, and tore my shirt.

A guard with a flashlight appeared. Bobby was terrified. He held the stiletto against my ribs and kept threatening me. I whispered not to worry. As the guard walked by, Bobby and I lay still as statues.

This was the turning point. Bobby made no more physical advances. He couldn't understand why I failed to respond the way he expected. My continuing to treat him as a friend threw him off balance.

We talked for most of the night. At one point I lay my hand gently on his chest while he told me about his loneliness. Finally he cried a little. He said it was the first time he'd cried since he was a child. By the time the guard came through again we were both lying quietly awake but no longer talking. Not long after that I fell asleep.

The next morning I was tired but elated. I was released before breakfast and never saw or heard from Bobby again.

This and similar experiences lead to specific suggestions for the conduct of nonviolent self-defense.

1. BE CLEAR ABOUT YOUR OBJECTIVES: I didn't want to get hurt and didn't want to submit to Bobby sexually. In addition, I didn't want to hurt or humiliate him. The basis of my defense was to communicate this.

2. DON'T BE FRIGHTENED: Your fear communicates itself directly and eggs on your opponent. What helped me most was keeping an intense focus on Bobby. If fear wells up, breathe deeply. Keep talking. Maintain as much eye contact as possible without being threatened.

3. DON'T BE FRIGHTENING: When nonviolent defense fails, this is most often the reason. Someone committing an act of violence is likely to be full of fear, ready to respond explosively to the slightest thing. The most dangerous moment with Bobby was when the guard appeared. Any unexpected noise or movement could have caused him to stab me reflexively. Make no abrupt gestures. Move slowly. When practical, tell your opponent what you are going to do before you do it.

4. DON'T AVOID STATING THE OBVIOUS: Tell your opponent how you're feeling. A statement such as "You're pulling my hair—it hurts" can have amazing results.

5. DON'T BEHAVE LIKE A VICTIM: Someone committing an act of violence has strong expectations of how the victim will behave. When I didn't behave the way Bobby expected, he was at a loss. The way of nonviolent defense is to create a scenario new to your opponent.

6. SEEK TO BEFRIEND YOUR OPPONENT'S BETTER NATURE: My defense against Bobby worked because I saw and made contact with parts of him I genuinely liked and admired. If I saw him only as brutal and loathsome, nonviolent defense would have been more difficult, if not impossible.

7. RESIST PHYSICALLY AS FIRMLY AS YOU CAN WITHOUT ESCALATING THE ANGER OR VIOLENCE: Watching others experiment with nonviolent defense, the most frequent mistake has been not resisting firmly enough. Sometimes passivity— particularly during a rape—further angers or excites your opponent. On the other hand, your opponent might be so

overwrought that even a mild form of physical resistance can backfire explosively. You have to play it by ear.
8. KEEP TALKING, KEEP LISTENING: Get your opponent talking. Really listen. Don't argue, but at the same time don't give the impression you agree when you don't. Listening is more important than what you say. Keep confrontation verbal and outlast your opponent.

Gene Knudsen-Hoffman:

A PROPOSAL FOR THE CRIMINAL AND THE INSANE

One of my daughters spent a summer working in an American Friends Service Committee work camp in Connecticut. Under the auspices of a psychiatrist, sixteen college students were paired with sixteen back-ward (this meant hopeless) patients from the state mental hospital. My daughter was teamed with a schizophrenic patient.

They took the patients camping for six weeks. The patients were expected to set up tents, prepare food, dig the latrines, and perform other chores just like the students.

My daughter said that in the beginning patients behaved strangely. When they were setting up camp one of the patients was hallucinating that he was Jesus; others were helpless, or angry, or withdrawn. But the camp setup continued as though everything were normal.

The students and their companions spent a lot of time together. My daughter, Valley, said that near the end of camp it was hard to tell who were the patients and who were the students, the improvement was so great. When the camp was over, some of the patients were dismissed as cured. Others, not so fortunate, were returned to the facility. Valley heard later that those who returned did not fare so well; when they were denied freedom and close companionship of the healthy, they regressed.

If we see that life is sacred, that punishment simply brings on more punishment, what does compassion say to us about the mad and the criminal?

I think it says very simply that restraint is necessary, but not punishment. Each person deserves an opportunity to repent as well as an opportunity to be healed. Prison does not usually heal people, nor does execution—neither the criminal nor those who want to kill him. I have worked with patients from state and county psychiatric facilities which were little different from prison. The patients certainly felt punished. Putting such people out on the streets, letting them fend for themselves in an inhospitable and frightened world, is another form of punishment.

What then might we do? We could build living facilities where people who care (and there are many of them) will seek to bring new life and learning to those we call insane or criminal. These would be centers of true rehabilitation (which means to restore to good condition) for people who may show us that loving creates love, and offering responsibility in such an environment creates responsibility.

And if and when these people are returned to society, what might they tell us of the causes of their unacceptable and antisocial behavior? Might they not become healers for the rest of us?

A police force of former criminals would certainly understand persons who commit a crime and might be able to help them without fear and intimidation and threat. Many of the great healers in the world have been the wounded ones themselves.

This could be a new way to release that creative potential which dwells in each of us.

Sister Ann Marie Quinlan IHM:

IMAGINE...THE DEATH PENALTY

To really enter the problem, I imagined myself on Death Row, recovered from the brief amnesia during which I apparently killed someone. After much prayer and pondering, I asked to visit the inmate of each cell in our infamous block. These contacts convinced me that a good third of our number were mentally handicapped, and another somewhat overlapping third had histories of emotional instability. The rest were mostly victims of childhood poverty and abuse and, later, desperation and drugs.

If we had been lifers, I could visualize a great long-term program. But even for whatever time we had left, my experiment would be worth trying. Why couldn't I persuade nutritionists, doctors, psychologists, or handicap specialists of my own acquaintance to work with us to help create and implement a three-pronged program for the low IQs, the emotionally unstable, and our poorly nourished, uncared for, uneducated, and addicted people. In our rag-tag community some would be patient enough to bring the educable up a few notches. Some seemed strong enough to pair off with the emotionally unstable, and many of us could learn to develop skills useful for ourselves and for making some atonement.

Our little campaign of self-transformation as responsible citizens might change enough Florida voters' hearts to get the death penalty abolished down here.

With the money they'd save from executions, we could go far in rehabilitation.

Imagine...

PERSONAL

Masha Soloveyschik:

UNDERSTANDING EACH OTHER'S PAIN

I think that people who want war simply do not know what warmth and happiness are. They seek satisfaction in striving for power. When I read American books on psychology, I see clearly that all people have common problems. In the whole world people suffer from loneliness, from not being able to love and be loved, from being overwhelmed with problems of childrearing and the complex problems of parent relationship.

Could it be possible to have International Psychotherapeutic meetings?—without having to discuss or solve problems of war and peace? We could just simply talk about our problems, about what is bothering us. Only then can we see how many feelings we share and how little we differ.

Only in this way can we begin to feel for each other and understand the other nation's pain. Only then will we be able to not argue any longer!

David Hoffman:

AFTER THE FEAR IS GONE

The solution to humanity's shared predicament of living under the threat of nuclear war can be found only through a radical transformation of human consciousness. No amount of moralizing about the issue will suffice; nor will any tinkering with missile systems or additional data about the relative strengths of opposing armies. It doesn't help to blame anyone or any country. It doesn't matter who is right or wrong. The problem with our warring tendencies is a profound one; and the remedy, of necessity, will require changes that are both psychological and spiritual.

The method is not very different from that which has been so successfully employed by Alcoholics Anonymous. The first step entails a surrendering to the problem, and to our helplessness: nuclear war is simply unpreventable. The acknowledgement presupposes a willingness to fully experience our grief, anger, and despair. Since what we repress in ourselves we eventually project elsewhere and onto others, it is literally true that, ultimately, people get what they fear.

In our submission to the unpreventability of nuclear war, we eventually come to drop the notion of "Us versus The Bomb" and discover we are part of a larger system that includes both the bomb *and* us. So long as it's the Russians or the Pentagon or whoever, the problem is not fully ours and we remain on the sidelines with our anger and our fears. But because we are part of the larger system that includes all this, we can change that system by changing ourselves.

In letting go of our resistance, we give up not only our

personal guilt and self blame, but we give up blaming others, and also learn what it is that *attracts* us to the source of our fears. If we perceive only the horrors of war, we fail to understand the purposes it fulfills and the fascination it holds for us. It does no good trying to turn away from that to which we are drawn and even addicted. Instead of repressing symptoms, we need to understand their cause. And even more important, we must start to invent some workable alternatives. This involves our learning to appreciate the differences opposing cultures represent to each other, rather than fearing those differences and attempting to destroy them through the vehicle of war.

Such a vision can develop only from a perspective and strategy that are nonpartisan. This is not to be confused with *"uncritical."* Rather, the nonpartisan mind is one that transcends the limits of any ideological thinking which claims exclusive rights to the truth.

Under the shadow of the bomb, we are like plants that strain for survival. Together we seek out the sun where we can find it. Nothing has united our planet more than the common threat of nuclear annihilation.

Equally important, though, must be our acknowledgment that we are incapable of changing the world unless we transform ourselves in the process. In confronting the threat of nuclear war, we have discovered that it is not really the bomb which threatens us, but *people*. The bomb is a product of our imagination and the war is within us. Our tendency to fear our hardware or blame others for our predicament is merely symptomatic of a sense of powerlessness as individuals in the modern state. But *networking*, a new process, alters this presumption as we recognize that we *can* change the world because we are an interwoven part of its fabric.

We are a network by virtue of our personal relations and shared philosophy. This is a stance beyond the partisan and the dogmatic. It is one that seeks truth in the dispassionate understanding of another's point of view, appreciates difference, and scatters authority. Its roots are rational and emotional, subconscious and spiritual. And it offers a form through which humanity can realize those self-transformations that are now essential to the survival of the planet.

Robert Fuller:

EVERYBODY'S WORK

Five hundred years before Christ, Mo Tzu taught universal love and put forward the notion that one should love all human beings equally. During the time in Chinese history known as the Warring States period, Mo Tzu and his followers would travel on foot to sites of developing conflict and attempt a kind of diplomatic *aikido*. If the opposing parties would not agree to mediate their dispute, Mo Tzu would join the weaker side, offer training in how to withstand a siege, and then again appeal for a negotiated solution. His willingness to commit himself *personally* to a vision of a world free of war serves as a source of inspiration to citizen diplomats who today, in ever greater numbers, are resuming his work.

Anyone may carry the Mo Tzu banner. Motzuing seldom takes the form of actually mediating an internal or intergroup conflict.

The final details of peacemaking necessarily fall to the official (partisan) participants themselves. But *there is another prior job: that of creating conditions favorable to negotiation.* Sometimes this takes the form of the negotiators' willingness to meet; sometimes it takes the form of altering the format, or the context, of the negotiations.

Almost always it involves improving communications between the citizens of the two groups whose governments are in conflict.

It is a distinct advantage not to be identified as a spokesperson for a government or even an institution. As a free agent you are at liberty to say the "outrageous things" that often need saying. You can invite people to explore positions they would feel obliged to refuse to consider if presented officially.

While the contributions of Motzuing to official diplomacy can be important, there is perhaps a more profound consequence of citizen diplomacy, which in the 1980s, for the first time in history, has seen thousands of ordinary citizens do their part to better international communications and relations.

Today war is no longer a spectator sport—everyone is forced into the role of participant, and death is very likely. In this context, the issues of war and peace are too important to be left to the politicians. We must take responsibility for creating peace ourselves. The goal is to create conditions among the peoples of the world which permit and require the official diplomats to negotiate the final peace treaties.

With tens of thousands of citizens travelling to foreign lands, Motzuing translates into people knowing their "enemy" and transforming that enemy and themselves into partners. The old game of War is superseded by the new game—call it Completion. The peoples of the world's societies complete and thereby transform and empower themselves by incorporating into themselves the truths that other societies embody and exemplify. Doing Mo Tzu work is guided by the strategy of "finding love in what you hate."

So, in looking at African, Islamic, or Russian culture, the task is to identify that aspect of truth each bears most prominently. Our initial reaction to people is often negative because they fail to embody something we think is supremely important. At first we may experience them as wrong-headed, inefficient—and it's true, often they are inept in areas where we excel. Eventually we may understand that through their "weaknesses" they are protecting certain insights which contribute to their uniqueness, their essential gift for the rest of us.

To see what such qualities are, and to find another way of

seeing and being with our own, is the work before us. *Vive la difference* is the best anti-war cry imaginable.

In this game of Completion there appears another outline, coaxing us away from the thrills of the battlefield. There is nothing the world needs more than nonpartisans who are willing to see their own culture and a rival one as complementary, as each bearing an aspect of a larger truth, a truth that embraces both and compromises the essential character of neither.

The linchpin of forbearance for another people is to identify the truth or value their culture has borne forward through its particular history. The key to evoking a reciprocal respect is to know the truths exemplified by our own culture.

Everyone must find what they love in what they may at first be inclined to hate. Only then can different cultures truly meet, and human beings be enabled to complete themselves.

Jonathan Sisson:

THE WORLD AS A GLASS BOTTLE

An encounter with Danilo Dolci: tall and heavily built, Danilo Dolci is an imposing figure.

His very size is surprising for a man who became famous because of his fasting on behalf of the rural poor in Sicily.

Now he is seated in front of a large audience at Wartensee, a center for adult education located in an old Swiss castle. Before he begins to speak he holds up a glass bottle for all to see, and then hands it to the person sitting nearest him. The bottle passes from hand to hand around the room. Strangely disfigured, the originally green-colored glass shows streaks of molten red and orange. A few Japanese characters are still visible on the surface. Taking it in his hands again, he begins to speak: "If we don't want to become like this bottle, then we have to change our way of life . . ."

A few days later I had the opportunity of talking with Danilo Dolci for several hours. "Experience is necessary," he told me, "in order to find out where change is possible. Without a basis in experience all our thoughts [about a nonviolent future] are unrealistic and become nothing more than dreams."

I thought of the bottle from Hiroshima. I was moved by the silence at the beginning of his talk and sensed the perplexity of many who took the bottle into their hands—some with horror, others with reverence. And so I asked him why he had begun by handing the bottle around the room, an act which I interpreted as symbolic. The answer, in its essence, was simple and profound: "If such a bottle is placed in your hands," he explained, "and you understand its meaning, then you have understood something which will stay with you for the rest of your life."

He then told me about a visitor from Japan. He was a survivor of the Hiroshima bombing, had brought the bottle with him and shown it to the children during a class period. The next day a parent told Danilo that his son had understood everything. Danilo asked him what the child had understood. "My son told me," the parent continued, "if we don't pay attention, the world is going to turn into a melted glass bottle." (Danilo asked himself then: If a six-year old child was able to draw this conclusion after a single lesson, why should grown men and women twenty—thirty—fourty years old and older, not be able to do the same?)

For Danilo Dolci, this is an example of what he calls a "basis in experience." To my objection that it is one thing to understand an event and its possible ramifications ("Even a six-year old child is capable of that") it is something else to draw conclusions based upon that and apply them to one's own sphere of activity, he responded by saying that we must learn to develop alternatives. The tools which enable us to develop alternatives are observation and analysis. Yet, how do we translate observation and analysis into a viable solution? Danilo Dolci once discussed this question with Daniel Berrigan. In one respect, it is easy to pound missile components with a hammer, as the Berrigan brothers did in a General Electric weapons factory. The more difficult task, however, is to offer the workers in that factory an alternate means of occupation. What alternatives exist for the peasants who grow poppy and coca and depend upon a market for opium and cocaine to earn their living? What other choice does the young campesino have who joins the national guard as a soldier or the contras as a mercenary?

In response, Danilo Dolci gave another example. The bandits in Partinico are notorious as vicious thieves. Danilo knew one such bandit who used to stand at a curve on a mountain road and rob automobiles. When construction was begun on the dam in Partinico, the bandit was one of the first to show up for work. Danilo was surprised and asked him about it. The bandit's answer was simple: "Stealing is much too dangerous," he said, "when there is work like this to do."

"In Partinico," said Danilo Dolci, "we never talked about nonviolence."

George Zabelka:

A CALL TO ACCOUNTABILITY

I am a Roman Catholic priest. I served as Catholic Chaplain for the personnel of the 509th Composite Group (the atomic bomb group in 1945) in July and August. I had mass and other services for them both on Sundays and weekdays.

I made a terrible mistake. I was "had" by the father of lies. I

PERSONAL

participated in the big "ecumenical" lie of the Catholic, Protestant, and Orthodox churches. I wore the uniform. I was part of the system. I painted a machine gun in the loving hands of the nonviolent Jesus, and then handed this perverse picture to the world as the truth. As Catholic Chaplain, I was the final channel that communicated this fraudulent image of Christ to the crews of the Enola Gay and the Bocks Car.

"I was wrong." Christ would not be the instrument to unleash such horror on his people. Therefore no follower of Christ can legitimately unleash the horror of war on God's people.

"I was wrong." To say otherwise would be to bypass the first and absolutely essential step in the process of repentance and reconciliation—admission of error.

I would like to ask the universal church—Catholic, Orthodox, Protestant—to stop making war respectable. For the last 1,700 years the church has been making not only war respectable, it has been inducing people to believe that it is an honorable Christian profession. We have been brainwashed. The soldier by profession is a paid, professional killer. The gospel of the just war is a gospel Jesus never taught. War is now, always has been and always will be bad news.

I would like to insist, with the urgency with which a mother warns her child about a lethal danger, that the issue for the church is not nuclear war, but the total and unequivocal rejection in theory and practice of all war and mass slaughter.

Let's get it straight...

No one in the early, nonviolent church ever taught that Christians were to ignore evil. The Christian was to overcome evil with good and, if called upon, give his or her life for the early church (martyrdom was a major social activity). To "lay down one's life" (not to kill another) in responding to evil was seen as the ultimate act of social responsibility.

Serious social responsibility required more than saying "I am against war." Verbal opposition to grave evil may be better than no option, but it is low-voltage discipleship. The early Christian spirituality of speaking up clearly and paying up personally is light years away from an ethic that justifies participating in evil and then participating in it until *all agree not to participate in it.*

I call upon people to make their voices heard in our world. We can no longer leave this to our leaders, either political or religious. They will move when we make them move. They represent *us.* Let us tell them that they must think and act for the safety and security of all people in our world.

Again I call for a truly ecumenical council of world religious leaders to state clearly that war is a crime against God and humanity. Our religious leaders must state that each of us becomes responsible for the crime of war by cooperation in its preparation and execution.

Today we are worshipping the god of metal: the bomb. We are putting our trust in physical power, militarism, and nationalism. I, too, am a prophet, though a reluctant one.

We must all become prophets. We *must all do something for peace.* We can all live together as brothers and sisters, or we are doomed to die together as fools in a world holocaust.

Ronald Beasley

THE LITURGY PROTEST

There is increasing concern about the appropriateness of civil disobedience—or, as some would say, "holy obedience"—when it requires Christians to disobey the law. Whether this is cutting the wire, standing in front of a military convoy, or refusing to pay tax, some Christians, though convinced about the objective (banishing nuclear weapons forever), also remain unconvinced about the means.

Meanwhile, the urgency of achieving the objective remains.

Therefore, maybe Christians in particular should look at their own liturgical lifestyle to see how it could be brought to bear as an influence for good which will help in the process of banishing nuclear weapons forever. Here are two suggestions.

Prayer is the lifeblood of the Christian. By this, I mean the vibrant sensitivity which links us to the very "ground of reality" and puts us in deep touch with the "infinite." Christians could use their discipline of prayer in the anti-nuclear campaign, but more overtly than is usually expected. Because of its importance and because of the need to show a significant symbol, Christians could willingly, once a week, abdicate from their daily work, and remain at home for a day in prayer and meditation, focusing on the struggle against militarism. They could indicate openly to their employer that they will be absent tomorrow because they will be spending the day praying for peace.

It would be important to take a day regularly to pray rather than work—a day's salary would be forfeited. And if the churches were mobilized, we could have thousands of women and men staying off work one day a week for peace.

To take it one step further, there could be a national timetable of the days to be taken off so that, in effect, the embargo would be effectively demonstrated somewhere every working day. It would be essential for it to be done quietly, at home, and in small groups. The witness and the effect could be significant.

A second strategy might be to take account of the starving millions who exist because we spend money on expensive nuclear arsenals, leaving the poor and the hungry across the world to die. While this situation exists, should not every Christian renounce the opportunity of the Eucharist?

How can we share the bread and wine—the Body and Blood of Christ—while women and men and children die because they lack food and we will not provide it for them? Our liturgy is made an obscenity and a blasphemy.

Here in Scotland, the General Assembly of the Church of Scotland agreed recently that congregations should set up peace groups. The tasks outlined here could be the kernel of any church peace group. Christians could show how, by using their liturgy, they can in a constructive way demonstrate their dissident view against rampant militarism—at least here in Scotland.

If we had the will to do it, the sufferers from militarism and spiritual hunger would perceive a new dimension of spiritual protest grounded in conviction and faith. Yes, it would turn the Church inside-out. But if it also overturned the power of militarism, I for one would be certain the price paid was worth it.

David H. Albert:

ACCUMULATORS ANONYMOUS

There is a professor who believes he has discovered that the earliest form of primitive accumulation took place in the form of beer. So-called primitive human beings came upon the fact that gathered grains, when fermented, could be stored in liquid form, thus allowing hunting and gathering activity to progress beyond the bare subsistence level.

I have no idea whether the professor is correct and am not waiting with anticipation to find out. But the metaphor of "drunken accumulation," or, more precisely, an "addiction to drunken accumulation," seems an apt one for our time.

I do not know what new innovation, what new turn of consciousness, can lead us out of the global catastrophe we and all other peoples on earth—the tree people, the sea people, the animal people—are already suffering. I do not imagine such a panacea exists at this time. But even if it did, even within the pages of this book, I can't imagine how we humans—addicted as we seem to be to drunken accumulation, and consumed with defending it—could recognize such a panacea for what it is, even if we saw it.

I take it as a given that, within the context of the contemporary military-industrial state, we act—or at least stand in complicity with—systems and modes of existence which result in the death, injury, suffering, and oppression of other human beings, the wholesale destruction and pollution of the natural environment, and the extermination of species who have claims upon the earth at least equal to our own. Virtually everyone represented in this book I'm sure recognizes that fact, and yet our addiction prevents us from thinking or even feeling clearly and stunts our imaginations as to the proper course of action to take.

But, until we as individuals find ways to become sober, to withdraw from our addictions to accumulation and to the military-industrial state, and until we as a society overcome our addiction to empire and lifestyles which empire supports, our efforts will be blunted if not still-born. It's premature even to discuss the merits of "peace exchanges," peace-oriented "game theory," particular unilateral initiatives, or even the application of forms of meditation as ways out of our nightmare. Until we are sober, or at least on the path to recovering our shriveled selves, we will have no sound method of evaluating their relative effectiveness.

So, as a beginning, I think we should take to heart the words of Nancy Reagan: "Just say no!" Let all peace initiatives and peace group discussions begin as sections of Accumulators Anonymous, with individuals admitting their own peculiar addiction to accumulation and the military state, how it has stunted their own growth as full human beings, and what small steps they have taken to withdraw from cooperation with the system which would annihilate us all.

Let professors talk about how much money their universities receive from the government and from the military, and how they personally benefit from it, and how they are beginning to say no. Let taxpayers talk about how fond they are of their personal property, and how they are beginning to include notes of protest with their tax payments, or are beginning to withhold even small amounts from what they are presumed to owe for their own destructions. Let homeowners talk about that which they own and never use, and how they are taking steps to dispossess themselves of what they don't need so that those without do not have to suffer want. Let our community and church groups become loci of community therapy.

I would make it clear that I don't believe this community therapy will be a sufficient step to usher in an age of peace, only a necessary one. It may be possible that a drunken driver might get us to our destination, but I'd rather bet on a sober one.

Pat Farren:

NONVIOLENT POWER TAKES NONVIOLENT PEOPLE

For the past decade I've worked at two jobs that have a lot in common—editing a journal on peace and social justice, and, with my spouse, caring for a family that has grown to include three young people.

The deadlines and the diapers, the layout and the cuddling, the typos and the toddlers are connected by nonviolence. The macro-issues of the newsletter and the micro-issues of my parenting both involve nurturing—promoting the development of fragile, sacred human lives.

Our youngest, our baby, was diagnosed at three months old as suffering from a liver disease that would probably be fatal. We spent half a year weeping and praying for him, coming to value more acutely his every day, before tests revealed that his particular condition was benign and would heal with the passage of time. Now, upon reading in the newspaper of other youngsters facing liver transplants (with their 50 percent survival rate), I cry for the pain they and their families must endure.

My experiences in the Peace Corps and in my peace work have taught me that our world is filled with far more suffering, many more dying children and anguished adults, than most people are able to admit. To be fully human is to be a bleeding heart.

Making nonviolence transform major national and international situations requires a conceptual wholeness that cannot be realized globally until we learn to act on it locally. Nonviolence is a love story that must be told in our homes before it's going to take hold across our planet.

I deal in both my jobs with the nitty-gritty of nonviolence, not so much with the theory. Increasingly I am coming to realize that I cannot credibly recommend international harmony when my own heart is in chaos, nor express real solidarity with the oppressed when I am blocked from love with my immediate family. When I'm angry with my spouse, it's hard to feel gentle toward my colleagues. When I've come from yelling at a daughter, it's almost impossible to move toward reconciliation with those who fund the mercenaries and build the weapons.

Violence—the violence of the state and of the spirit—is a kind of addiction. While the military people and the policymakers may be the major dealers of the drug, many of us are addicted. Abstinence—laying down the addiction and going cold-turkey vulnerable on a day-to-day basis—can feel profoundly threatening. We probably need support groups to help liberate us: affinity groups, a sense of community with others in withdrawal.

We can freeze and reverse the nuclear arms race only by freezing and reversing our violence of spirit; resist imperialism effectively only after releasing those dominated in our own circles; disconnect the deadly connection by love alone.

Demonstrations of personal caring must accompany our street demonstrations. Direct actions of solidarity with those in pain can bring integrity to our witnesses on behalf of more distant victims. Negotiations around the kitchen table must precede those around the conference table. Practicing nonviolence is like practicing a sport or other discipline—getting good at it requires making it a conscious pursuit, an exercise worked at daily with a fierce, gentle persistence.

The enormous moral force of nonviolence can become the central social reality of the coming century not by coercion or by logic alone, but by example. Nonviolence can't save the world. Only nonviolent people can.

Gene Knudsen-Hoffman:

DAYS OF NONCOOPERATION

In the days when I first became a pacifist we used to speculate on what we'd do if the Nazis invaded us or the Communists came "walking down our streets." One solution, we decided, would be noncooperation—to make our society non-functional. "Nobody," we said, "could conquer us if we didn't cooperate."

Well, we *have* been invaded and occupied by the military: by thousands of nuclear weapons and by ever-growing piles of nuclear waste—but most of all, by fear.

What might happen if we decided that we wouldn't cooperate with a life that's streaming toward destruction? What if we said a gigantic "no" to make way for a greater "yes"? What if we brought to a halt the wheels that grease the smoothness of our daily lives?

This would mean sacrifice and suffering, and it is no easy task. We would need to organize so well that we could care for and support one another. But I think of what it would be like if there were nuclear war: no garbage pick-up—no garbage; no bathing of babies—no babies; no teenagers yearning after the heroic—no teenagers; no mothers, no fathers, no grandparents—nobody. No body.

Can you imagine living in a world with nobody? No trees? No flowers? A world without a cookie and a glass of milk, without a band-aid?

Well, it doesn't have to be. We can stop it. We could begin with one hour of noncooperation. We could go to work one hour late and during that time we could vigil at some public place bearing banners that say NO WORK WITHOUT DISARMAMENT. Little by little we could increase the times of noncooperation. Who knows what a month, when citizens refuse to work on Mondays, would do?

How can we accomplish any of this? By joining with other like-minded people and planning small actions. If we had twenty-five such small affinity groups Santa Barbara, say, would soon be "Peace City."

And finally, when we meet with opposition (as we surely will), and when it's violent, I hope we'll be grounded deeply enough in nonviolence to be able to sing to them:

> May the long-time sun shine upon you
> All love surround you;
> And the pure light within you
> Guide your way on.

Amos Gvirtz:

THOUGHTS ABOUT CONSTRUCTIVE PROTEST

When one considers modern societies, I think it is possible and helpful to compare them to the patriarchal families of today. In our modern societies, we have governments that are responsible for the needs of society, both internally and externally. Citizens relate to their governments like families relate to their parents. Indeed, there is a kind of hierarchical system of society and government that can be compared to that of the family.

We in the peace movements are known to be very critical of our governments. We are therefore critical of those who act toward us like parents in a family, and we are heard to say that these 'parents' are bad. For some time I have thought that it is curious that the governments of the world react to the peace movement so negatively. Perhaps it is because we are saying to these "parents," these 'governments,' that they are bad. The negative reaction we receive from them is not a result of the fact that *we* are bad (which we are not) nor is it a result of a negative reaction to our ideas. I believe this negative reaction is because our governments perceive us to be critical of the symbols of self-identity—the government of our own society.

The peace movements in the West are generally led by people with busy lives—often middle-class people who engage in peace activities in their spare time. Often these people have bad consciences, and their involvement is simply to "clean" their conscience. We must progress beyond this to a new orientation of effectiveness and success, not merely to make ourselves feel better. To be more successful we must make our suggestions and criticisms in a way that is not the shouting of more troublemakers, but the responsible search for better ways to relate to each other in the world.

Let us consider one of the basic "tools" of the peace movement—the demonstration.

We demonstrate because we want the authorities to do what we want and not what they are currently doing. After we demonstrate for our wishes we go home and leave the hard work to the authorities—especially the hard work of implementing the suggestions we have made. In fact, up to a certain level (actual revolution) such demonstrations will strengthen the authority of the government, since it implies that we, the demonstrators, still recognize their authority and expect *them* to change and be better authorities. This means that we haven't taken responsibility ourselves, only made demands.

The alternative approach is what I call "constructive protest." Constructive protest means that we take upon ourselves the responsibility to move and act on our own suggestions, our own demands. It can have the following positive effects: (1) constructive protest serves as a warning to authorities that if there is no change, they may well lose their responsibility and authority. (This is the element of pressure inherent in the method.) (2) Constructive protest means that the protestors will appeal to the public at large as responsible persons and not as troublemakers.

For example, governments are often engaged in creating "facts"—facts of war such as weapons, and (as in Israel), settlements on occupied land. These "facts" are elements that encourage wars to happen.

Yet in the peace movement we almost never create different or alternative "facts of peace." A fact of peace would be the direct application of an alternative method of dealing with those social realities that the facts of war were created to deal with. A fact of peace is an alternative.

In Israel, Neve Shalom (Oasis of Peace) is an experimental village where Arabs and Jews live together of their own free choice. Such a fact of peace is a means of making our claims relevant to a public that often does not listen—or that even openly hates our message, such as workers and the poor in a society like Israel. For such people, the peace movement has not succeeded in being relevant. We must learn from peace movements in the Third World. The peace movement must work in poorer neighborhoods to make peace visions relevant for them. For example, if we oppose the weapons factories and what they are, the peace movement must suggest practical alternative employment for workers in those factories. What we need are practical suggestions, not words of protest.

Finally, consider the economic influence of the arms industries and all others associated with creating facts of war. We can see more and more how the military-industrial complex dictates to government authorities in such a way that limits choices—in short, the complex governs *for* them by giving them very little choice. Constructive protest can create a new alliance between the peace movement and government precisely by creating new alternatives—new choices—and therefore strengthening government to make the choice for peace.

James Forest:

BREAKING UP A RIOT

In the early 70s, I worked with a project called the Quaker Project on Community Conflict (QPCC). Not all of us were Quakers; I was the one Catholic; there were at least two Jews. Among the things we had in common was an affection for granola, which we ate with yogurt and honey. It was sometimes said that we were working for the Granola Project on Quaker Conflict.

Our office was a storefront on the lower East Side in Manhattan, and from this base we arranged quite a lot of non-violent training seminars. Perhaps of more immediate importance to New York was work we were doing in riot situations.

Several lessons have stuck with me ever since. One is the power of names.

It was a time when gays were beginning to "come out of the closet." Some anti-gays came out as well, as a result of which gay meeting points in Greenwich Village became the site of several serious assaults on gays. The gays realized that they needed to learn to defend themselves. Some argued there was no effective alternative but violence and proposed gays take some training in counter-assault. Others maintained that nonviolence could be as or more effective. As a result, some training sessions involving the staff of QPCC were arranged.

The sessions went well. The results were quickly put to the test. I can recall one summer night in Greenwich Village when we seemed a few minutes away from a riot involving gay people and a crowd of hostile straights who had come down to the village to "bash queers." Some nasty names were being shouted, especially by the straights, though there was two-way verbal traffic. The two or three of the gays who had been involved with the nonviolence training went over to some of the people who were screaming and began introducing themselves and asking the names of the people they were facing. "Hello, my name is Bill Jones. What's yours?" The people they were talking to were surprised. Some responded with hostility—"I'm not talking to any queers"—but others responded by giving their own names. The gays asked, "Can you help us? We don't want anyone to get hurt but things are getting out of hand." A couple of conversations involving people on both sides sprang up. They weren't easy discussions. The straights were using words and phrases that were meant to explode like hand-grenades. But the gays managed to hold their own, avoiding throwing in their own verbal explosives, and within a quarter hour it was clear that the street atmosphere had changed dramatically. There was no riot.

At the next training session a few days later, there was a lot of discussion of what had happened that night. "Things changed when we offered our names," one of the gays said. "As soon as we had names we were people, and when they began giving us their names, they were as well.

Phil McManus:

BRIAN WILLSON AND
THE MUNITIONS TRAIN

In September 1987, a Vietnam War veteran was critically injured while blockading a train loaded with arms bound for Central America. Brian Willson had served in Vietnam before coming back disillusioned with U.S. policy. In February 1987, he risked death as part of an unarmed presence in the war zones of Nicaragua in protest of U.S. support for the *contras*. But it was here at home, at the hands of his own government, that his legs were cut off and his head crushed.

The action at the Concord Naval Weapons Station was part of a long and honorable tradition of peaceful protest in our country. The train made no attempt to stop, even though authorities were informed well in advance of the plans for the blockade. It is difficult to escape the conclusion that orders were given to run through the protesters and that the Navy was guilty of attempted manslaughter presumably in an attempt to end the ongoing demonstrations.

With good reason, the Concord protests are called the Nuremberg Actions. The Nuremberg tribunals in the aftermath of World War II established not only the right, but the responsibility, to impede the illegal actions of one's government. It is from Concord that the U.S. ships the vast majority of arms for its wars in Central America. The war against Nicaragua has been ruled illegal by the World Court. Our government drenches the lands of Central America in the blood of thousands in pursuit of a foreign policy gone berserk. Perhaps it is not surprising that it runs down those who confront it at home.

But clearly, it is the protesters who are acting legally, and the government in a criminal manner.

Grief and anger are appropriate responses to such a tragedy. Outrage should find expression in an insistence that the Navy be held legally accountable for its actions and in concerted protest against the policies which underlie them. But ultimately the source of our strength lies elsewhere. And we must tap that strength and put it into action if we hope to stop the train of death.

The train at Concord is a symptom of a deeper malady which we must confront. The train will run as long as our country is governed by fear, whether it is the crude fear of "anti-communism" or the callous fear of those who cling to their privilege and refuse to see that all people possess the same basic human dignity.

In the end, we will stop the train by changing a mentality. Before he was maimed, Brian Willson stated the matter in startling clarity: "One truth seems clear: If the munitions train moves past our blockade, other human beings will be killed and maimed. We are not worth more. They are not worth less."

This is the koan, the transparent riddle of our day. Neither our numbers, no matter how great, nor any amount of shouting, nor any court ruling will really bring it home to our compatriots (or ourselves). We are challenged to plumb the depths of our nonviolence and to make our own witness love-in-action.

The newspaper image is startling and discomfitting: a Vietnam vet who willingly, resolutely, placed himself in front of the train. We can grapple with the truth Brian lived out: "We are not worth more." We can seek to make it understood. We can make sure it is not forgotten. We can win the respect and overcome the hostility of those on the other side of the tracks. We can begin by respecting them and refusing to be hostile toward them. We can go ourselves to the tracks, again and again if need be. Willing to pay the price of being human, we share the vulnerability of those in Central America with no privilege to protect them.

Thich Nhat Hanh:

CAN YOU WRITE A LOVE LETTER TO YOUR CONGRESSMAN?

In the peace movement there is a lot of anger, frustration, and misunderstanding. Its members can write very good protest letters, but they are not yet able to write a love letter. We need to learn to write a letter to the Congress or to the President of the United States that they will want to read and not just throw away. The way we speak, the kind of understanding, the kind of language we use, should not turn people off. The President is a person like any of us.

Can the peace movement talk in loving speech, showing the way for peace? I think that will depend on whether the people in the peace movement can *be* peace. Because without *being* peace, we cannot do anything *for* peace. If we cannot smile, we cannot help other people to smile. If we are not peaceful, then we cannot contribute to the peace movement. Peacework means, first of all, being peace.

Peace Pilgrim:

THE POSITIVE APPROACH

In my work I have chosen the positive approach. I never think of myself as protesting against something, but rather as *witnessing for* harmonious living. Those who witness *for,* present solutions. Those who witness *against,* usually do not. They dwell on what is wrong, resorting to judgment and criticism, and sometimes even to name-calling.

Naturally, the negative approach has a detrimental effect on the person who uses it, while the positive approach has a good effect.

When an evil is attacked, the evil mobilizes, although it may have been weak and unorganized before, and therefore the attack gives it validity and strength. When there is no attack, but instead good influences are brought to bear upon the situation, not only does the evil tend to fade away, but the evildoer tends to be transformed.

The positive approach inspires; the negative approach makes angry.

Juliet Hills:

TAKING PEOPLE SERIOUSLY

American freedom—to live, think, speak, and act without encroaching on other people—is world famous. All over this country there are serious, careful thinkers who live sensible lives. They eat carefully, drive safely, and avoid poisons, pollutants, and slick business deals. They are aware of the need for recognizing unity in and between all human societies, and they respect the prescientific knowledge of native cultures. They avoid television violence, they teach responsible thinking about war and nationality. They work in humanitarian jobs and read creative literature like this book. They live quietly, however.

There are unconscious forms of telling behavior, as well. Among the young in Europe, for example, people are anarchic, refusing to marry and introduce children into the nuclear apocalypse, writing rock songs about the rape of women and children, of consumers, and of the earth. They live noisily, however.

In a recent radio talk, I heard a responsible politician say the next generation will have the task of changing the apparent madness of world affairs. I disagree.

First, there is nothing sacred about health or youth. Ideals are easy to have. Having the courage to stand up for them and act in the community (and risk ridicule or loss of status) is another thing. More suited to age than youth.

Second, the buck stops with whoever is in a position to make a point. We already know people with whom we can be honest about our fears and hopes for responsible behavior in government or business. We all know people who amaze us with their clear moral system and courage to display it. Now it is *our* turn. It is our turn *now*.

We can suggest alternative behavior and thought to ourselves, our family and friends and colleagues. We can even suggest it to strangers, salespeople, public servants, health workers and church ministers.

Two problems are evident. The first is getting a sense of perspective, a philosophy of life that accommodates the facts of life. The world we live in is created, changed, and developed by us, either passively or actively.

The second problem is how to do it. We can use psychology to suggest how valuable someone else's help would be. We can invest people with a spoken trust that they rise to exhibit. We can say we would be unable to live with ourselves if we could not integrate our private morals with our professional behavior. We can also, of course, exhibit careful dealing with the people we know, and admit when we find it hard to handle situations. Exemplary behavior need not always imply criticism. It can be an honest expression of our awareness of the need to be firm, fair, generous, or perhaps even righteously angry or separate. It is usually more helpful to approach someone with an idea than to "tackle" them. And to remember what it would be like to be in their shoes.

Mary Evelyn Jegen, SND:

COMMON STOCK

A few days ago I was visiting Steve and Ava, a young couple who are in their second year of raising sheep for a living. Ava explained to me that this year they are not naming their lambs. Last year they gave each lamb a name. It made selling them for meat excruciatingly difficult.

I suggest a covert activity of naming each person we meet, whether we meet that person formally or in passing while going somewhere or even in our reading. We can give each person the lovely name "sister" or "brother." This is a most descriptive name, reminding us that our first identification is with the human race. Whoever our biological parents may be, in a very real way we are sprung from common stock.

Different religious and cultural traditions will invest the names sister and brother with different weights, different nuances of meaning. No matter. Recognizing each person as a sibling will make it immeasurably more difficult to entertain the peculiar and monstrous notion that it is tolerable to kill human beings to achieve the purposes of other human beings.

Chelli Glendinning:

THE PEACE-FAMILY TREE

The problem of nationalism persists—and with it state-supported enemy-making, politicking, military build-ups, wars, economic discrepancies, and cultural hegemony. Since deep and broadscale change occurs only when masses of people are touched in heartfelt ways, let us approach the problem of nationalism—not only at the negotiating table, in classrooms, and in the media—but also at the level of people's hearts. What if each and every person in the world were to have a "relation" from a different country?

Each person alive today could be assigned a relation now. We would be approximately the same age, but other factors (such as gender, race, occupation, and religion) could differ. A Peruvian shopkeeper could be linked to a German hausfrau, a Soviet diplomat to a Japanese priest, a U.S. welfare mother to a Philippine healer. Newborn babies could come into the world and, as with a godparent or sister, assume this relation as part of life and family. Everyone would have one. In fact, receiving one's relation could be ritualized as an initiation into global society.

The connection between these global relations would be based on mutual giving and respect. It could not, however, be based on the "foreign aid' model in which developed nations give money and "care" packages to developing peoples, freezing them into a one-down relationship of dependency. A Boston doctor may feel an important thing he can do for his relation (a laborer from Ghana) is to send food and medicine, yet he also understands that this factory worker has much to give him—the perspective of being Black in post-colonial Africá. A first question relations would ask of each other is: How can I know you? A second question is: How can I help you? A third question is: What can we teach each other?

Such a program could become an accepted and natural part of personal consciousness in the Nuclear Age, just as the nuclear family is today. Most exciting, it could become an accepted and natural part of global consciousness, linking people from all parts of the world and helping us see—from our own experience, in our hearts—that we share this planet together.

Floria Coon Teters, M.A.:

HOW TO STOP AN ARGUMENT

I t is a rare individual who does not want to be heard or who feels it is more meaningful not to have some impact on life. The changes we can bring about give us a sense of our value in society—whether the society is a family, community, group, or club. While acknowledging that the most critical issue today is nonviolence on a worldwide basis, it is also acknowledged that individuals must begin to think of alternatives to violence. That is the way norms develop in a society. One method that seems to be working successfully with couples and with parents and children is to condition the strongest member of the conflicted group to interrupt the developing argument by resisting the need to respond, and to ask *"What do we want to have come out of this?"*

The impending silence slows down the rate at which the argument is developing, and the question puts another focus to the argument. It also gives each a chance to state more clearly what is wanted. Often, what is wanted is not what the argument was about. It has been surprising how often couples, parents, and children have reported not knowing what they wanted, what the argument was about. Most acknowledged a need to win, to overpower, and that the anger came from elsewhere.

Frances Salant:

DERAILING VIOLENCE

A young friend of mine was part of a two-man voluntary civilian patrol in the Park Slope section of Brooklyn. He had been taught never to interfere in cases of "domestic" man-woman violence, but when he spotted a couple slugging it out on the sidewalk, he stopped the patrol car, got out, and approached the pair.

He dropped to all fours and barked like a dog. The fighters broke apart and fled in opposite directions. The unexpected and the ridiculous had de-railed the violence in which the two were immersed.

Sister Mary Evelyn Jegen, SND:

BENEVOLENT GLANCING

A small news item about Pope John Paul's visit to Southeast Asia a few years ago turned out to be a powerful impulse in my faith journey, and more specifically in my ongoing desire and effort to integrate prayer and other ways of working for peace. The news item told about the Pope's visit to the Supreme Patriarch of the Buddhists of Thailand. Protocol for that visit required that the two men sit together for a half hour in absolute silence, while they exchanged "benevolent glances." The story intrigued me. I wonder what it felt like to exchange benevolent glances with a stranger for a half hour.

Not long after I read the story, I decided to give it a try myself. Since I do not drive, I spend a fair amount of my life on public transportation. I made my first experiment on a Chicago bus. At first I felt a bit awkward. I did not try to engage anyone's eyes, so in effect the benevolent glancing was strictly a unilateral initiative. A strange thing happened. I found I was praying— not saying prayers, but being attentive, alert, and aware in a way impossible to describe. I was very much "with" a myste- rious depth of reality. I wanted to look with love. Love is what benevolence is all about, since the word benevolence means "to wish another well."

I never minded riding the bus; but since that first experience of benevolent glancing a few years ago, I look forward to bus riding as a great adventure, a genuine romance in the best sense of the word. As a matter of fact, if the day comes when I have no need to ride the bus, I firmly believe that I will ride anyway simply for the joy of benevolent glancing.

After about a year of practice, based solely on the authority of a one-and-a-half-inch newspaper story, I had the opportunity to check out my understanding with a Japanese Buddhist priest. He assured me that my interpretation of the newspaper story was basically correct. He then explained that the Buddhist way of seeing is very different from our Western approach. Wes- terners, he thought, seek to extract data, to "take" what they can from what they are looking at. A Buddhist is more apt simply to be present, to allow reality to present itself, to wait for it to come forward to meet the eye.

What has all this to do with peace? Very much, I think. Benevolent glancing is an art of attentiveness. Paying attention to what is before us is a way of prayer.

Benevolent glancing is relishing God by directly attending to what is immediately before us.

My experience has been that persons who would feel very uncomfortable in considering contemplative prayer as some-

58

thing for themselves (a pity to be so misinformed), can nevertheless become enthusiastic at the prospect of benevolent glancing.

Peacemaking and contemplation are so intimately related that one can hardly exist without the other. This truth can be appreciated by recognizing that violence depends on distorting the object or the victim of violence, turning the victim into an impersonal object which can be injured or even killed. An army officer told me that killing in war is easier today because soldiers do not have to look enemies in the eye as they are coming over the hill. Psychologically, it would be impossible to kill anyone on whom one had just been casting a loving glance. (Modern technology enables the killer to maintain a distance from the victim. In war-simulation exercises, when a target is bombed, the people in the vicinity are considered collateral damage—that is, burned, bleeding, and dead children, women, and men. It is impossible to cast a benevolent glance on "collateral damage.")

The day we teach people to look at the persons behind the abstraction, to glance benevolently at them, the military-industrial complex will have a very serious problem.

Erik Thorkild Hoffman:

TOOLS OF CHANGE

Many of us humans feel hopeless, stuck, static. In our hopelessness we lose sight that we have at our command the very tools that have bent the course of the world, the tools of all the great men and women that have altered the course of history, the tools of change. Let us examine these tools.

The first tool is our mind. It is in our mind that we conceive of the things we want to do. Our minds can roam the world or even the galaxy. Nikolas Tesla used his mind to build, test, debug, rebuild, and perfect his inventions before committing them to paper. Einstein travelled at the speed of light so he could see what light would look like standing still. C.S. Lewis went on flights of fancy through looking glasses. Thomas Jefferson postulated a world of equality, where men, and ultimately women, could freely voice their thoughts. All these people used their minds to conjure up the images and ideas they gave to the world, ideas that have profoundly changed the world we now live in.

The second tool we have is our voice. With our voice we can spread an idea. Ideas ripple outward from the center as the proverbial rock in water. From voice to voice an idea can move outward altering the thought patterns of those people who hear it. The slaves in our history sang songs to each other about freedom in the north. Teachers spread age-old thinking by voicing ancient ideas to their students. Lovers and friends give their most personal ideas to those close to them. These voices sow the seeds of change, seeds that may germinate into new ideas to be voiced.

What is a voice without ears? So ears are also tools of change. With our ears we hear the ideas voiced by others, ideas that then find a home in our minds. This establishes a beautiful circle of voice to ear to voice to ear. Ideas are expressed and feedback is given, allowing a honing of that idea. The very idea changes as it ripples outward in the sea of minds.

The last tool is our body. The mind gives the body the message and the body follows. By foot the mind moves, even as it wanders. With hands the body makes things. Evidence of these things are everywhere: buildings, cars, aluminum cans, campfire rings, bridges, and bombs. The mind controls the hands to make tools to gain greater control of the making of things. These things are the fruits of ideas, germinated in minds, and ripened by the hand.

These are the tools of change. We are each born with all, or most, of these tools intact, and can use them as we see fit. The sense of hopelessness that often invades us blinds us to our capacity to create change. All anyone needs to do is put these simple, time-tested tools to use.

A.C. Chikandamina:

TRAINING FOR PEACE

All nations need reorientation or education for peace. To most people, peace is good only if they have all they want (e.g., riches, political power, and power to defeat other nations). This has led the bigger powers to the arms race.

Peace movements should vigorously penetrate the educational systems of their countries to introduce peace education. Educating those in top posts of government alone does not work because any peaceful government can be pushed to violence by some violent elements in their country or in the neighboring states.

Peace movements therefore should invest mostly in peace-training projects rather than social projects. Most peace movements would support financially an economic social project. This trend has resulted in lots of money being spent on economic projects. But when conflicts arise in a country, all such projects are destroyed. If the money had been invested in peace initiatives, economic projects could develop without being destroyed.

Maurice Friedman, Ph.D:

DIALOGUE, TRUST, AND THE CONFIRMATION OF OTHERNESS

When marines shot a group of protesters in Manila a month or two ago, I heard a news commentator say that there had not been enough dialogue with the protesters. Unfortunately, this seems universally to be the case, and it is this which stands in the way of a movement toward building real community and real peace. "Only if humanity will be able to listen to justifiable though conflicting demands," writes the eminent family psychiatrist Ivan Bozormenyi-Nagy, "will it become fair to expect people to devote their energies to mutually sorting out their claims and alleged justifications. As long as indignant, ethnic, religious, racial groups find no ears to talk to, their energies are bound to be channeled into destruction."

To understand the human in community and society, we must make a distinction that is not usually made between two different types of community—the "community of affinity" and the "community of otherness." The community of affinity, or likemindedness, is based on what people feel they have in common—race, sex, religion, nationality, politics, a common formula, a common creed. The community of otherness, in contrast, does not mean that everyone does the same thing and certainly not that they do it from the same point of view. What makes community real is people finding themselves in a common situation—a situation which they approach in different ways, yet which calls each of them out. The very existence in genuine community is a common concern, a caring for one another. Community of affinity, or likemindedness, is always ultimately false community. Community of otherness, in contrast, is a way of being faithful and diverse at the same time.

The ultimate issue of the life of dialogue is community—lived togetherness of really unique persons, families, and groups. True community comes into being not through tolerance, adjustment, and compromise but through *mutual confirmation*.

No group is able to confirm all others. That is beyond human capacity. But the test of a fellowship is the otherness that it can confirm. It is our lack of trust, our existential mistrust, that makes us feel that we need to have the security of likeminded groups . . . rather than the concreteness of open meeting with real otherness that is present in every group, down to a pair of friends or a husband and wife.

Reconciliation depends upon each of us doing his or her share to build the "community of otherness." The respect for the otherness of the other does not mean I love everyone or even that I have resources to meet everyone in genuine dialogue. But it does mean that everyone who confronts me demands my attention and response—whether of love or hate, agreement or opposition, confirmation or merely letting be:

1. The greatest task that faces us is not to build enlightened utopias but to build peace in the context in which we find ourselves.
2. The true peacemakers are those who take upon themselves, in the most concrete manner conceivable, the task of discovering what can be done in each situation of tension and struggle by way of facing the real conflicts and working toward genuine reconciliation.
3. The knowledge that the others also witness for their "touchstones of reality" from where they stand can enable us to confirm the others in their truth even while opposing them.
4. We do not have to liberate the world from those who have different witnesses from us.
5. The imaginative task of comprehending a relationship from the other side as well as our own is essential to the goal of

overcoming war, for every war justifies itself by turning the enemy into a Manichaean figure of pure evil.

Dialogue means a meeting with the other person, the other group, the other people—a meeting that confirms the other yet does not deny oneself and the ground on which one stands. The choice is not *between* oneself and the other . . . rather, genuine dialogue is at once a confirmation of community *and* of otherness, and the acceptance of the fact that one cannot rise above that situation.

Every conflict has a least two sides. Even if one of the two sides is "dead wrong," it represents something real that cannot be done away with, namely, its existence.

All too often, the word "reconciliation" becomes associated with a sentimental good will that looks away from the very conflict that is to be reconciled or assumes that with this or that action or approach a tragic situation can be transformed into a harmonious one. Genuine reconciliation must begin with a fully realistic and fully honest recognition of real differences and points of conflict, and it must move from this recognition to the task of discovering the standpoint from which some real meeting may take place, a meeting which will include *both* of the conflicting points of view and will seek new and creative ways of reconciling them.

Genuine dialogue, whether between persons, groups, or nations, means holding your ground, but also, in opposing the other, confirming the other's right to stand where they do. We have been deluded by the notion that political power is the only power. We live in an age, God knows, in which the machines, the corporation, and the technocrat dominate to an incredible degree. Yet a real possibility remains, through standing one's ground, of bringing these back into human dialogue. If we are going to take this possibility seriously, then in each concrete situation we have to discover the hard way what the resources are for dialogue—interchange—so that humanity, at long last, "will be able to listen to justifiable, though conflicting, demands."

Michael Nagler:

MEDITATION AND THE CHALLENGE OF PEACE

It is because we have at the present moment everybody claiming the right of conscience without going through any disciplines whatsoever that there is so much untruth being delivered to a bewildered world. —M.K. GANDHI

Around Berkeley, California, one often hears, "If we only had a million people out there at Livermore we could stop the arms race." What this always makes me think is, what if we had one person who was a million times more committed?

A number of people concerned with peace and justice have come to feel that the interior dimension has been overlooked. We can use the analogy of the "new physics": As we thought of the physical world as separate bodies acting on one another primarily by collision, we thought of the social world too as changed only by coercive forces. An individual could not change such a system except by votes, or money, or violence. But scientists nowadays tend to think of the world as a field of forces, and it is much easier to see how the two might affect each other. It is not quite so fantastic that, as the Katha Upanishad says, "seated here in meditation, the Self moves all the world."

It is, however, possible to misunderstand this powerful truth. Many groups have sat beaming peace thoughts at the Pentagon without noticeable results; veering, as it were, from the apparent error of "politics only" to the counter-error of "nice thoughts only." It is not clear how the mind and the world interact or what we can do about it. Let me try to indicate my own view.

Adolf Hitler once boasted that he had rescued the German nation from its humiliation at the end of the first World War "by my fanatical will." There is nothing occult about this. The demented power of his will communicated itself to millions of people. And at the same time, by a peculiar irony, Gandhi was moving hundreds of millions in the precisely opposite direction.

It was the Mahatma's powerfully focused will which enabled him, in Martin Luther King's words, to "lift the love ethic of Jesus above mere interaction between individuals to a powerful and effective social force on a large scale."

The fact is, most of our resources lie locked up in the unconscious. Most of the power of the mind is not accessible to us by ordinary means. The power is closely connected with what Shaw and others called the Life Force. Our daily life—all the appetites, desires, thoughts, and activities—runs off the "interest" of this immense, largely unsuspected energy. By garnering carefully the energy available to him as to us, Gandhi was able to break through into the "principle," bringing untold resources to do good into his hands.

In a sense the mass media gives us access to deeper reserves of the mind's power than has been heretofore possible. But since no wisdom and no particular good will underlies the process, the media degrade the human image which each of us carries within and which so strongly determines how we think and act. The effect of the mass media goes far to explain why the peace movement is making so little headway; but in a negative way it also demonstrates that the crucial human predisposition toward peace and justice is alterable.

Meditation would enable us to reverse that mass media process; what group folly, motivated by greed, is driving asunder, individual discipline can pull back together. Where the social currents are slowly sweeping us back to barbarity, we can consciously wade forward, becoming each in our own way little Gandhis—and perhaps some of us becoming fairly big ones. As Storm Jameson, a British essayist, wrote: "All of us *wish* peace, but we do not *will* it." Through meditation we can will it. We can slowly recapture our will and bend its immense power to the cause we consciously approve of.

I hope I am conveying the difficulty of this task as well as the sense of hope it communicates. Thinking good thoughts is probably helpful, but certainly not the kind of force I am describing. The depth of psychological change I am referring to here cannot happen at an occasion. The battle has to be renewed every day—twice a day if one is going to be serious— and go on the rest of our life. It has little to do with pleasant thoughts, and many auxiliary disciplines have to be added to sustain this practice and realize its full effects.

In this conscious discipline, not only is immense personal power gradually added to us, but the wisdom and compassion to direct it. Where would Gandhi's charisma have gotten him without his uncanny shrewdness, the wonder of his friends and foes alike? By what he called conscious struggle to conserve his anger (thus converting it into compassion) he slowly brought his mind under control. This, I believe, gave him access to immensely deeper resources of psychological power.

Gandhi was able to direct his ever-growing energies efficiently to good—to his own sublime happiness, of which he leaves abundant testimony, and the supreme good of society. This will become evident to us, I believe, when we gather the strength to develop the complex legacy of his many experiments.

Mark Satin:

FROM JOBS TO "OWNWORK"

Democrats and Republicans, socialists and libertarians, are all calling for full employment. Their only bone of contention is who should create the jobs. The fact that the whole *point* of a post-industrial society is to reduce the "realm of necessity"; that millions of Americans would rather work part-time if they could, because they value family and friends more than status and things; that much of the actual work we do is not structured into paying "jobs"—none of this has yet entered into the calculations of our most learned economists.

In *Future Work: Jobs, Self-Employment and Leisure After the Industrial Age,* James Robertson sees three possible futures for work: maximizing employment, maximizing leisure, and maximizing self-directed work—what he calls "ownwork." These possible futures are not concocted out of thin air. They are based on three distinct perceptions of the future of industrial society, which Robertson calls, respectively, Business as Usual, HE (Hyper-Expansionist) and SHE (Sane, Humane, Ecological).

Robertson comes close to saying it's historically inevitable. "The SHE view of the future of work sees the historical progression from masters-and-slaves to lords-and-serfs and then to employers-and-employees as an unfinished progress toward greater equality. It now envisages a further step in that direction. As hopes of restoring full employment fade away, the dominant form of work will no longer be seen as employment but 'ownwork' . . .

"Ownwork means activity which is important and which

people organize and control for themselves. It may be either paid or unpaid. For the individual it may mean self-employment, essential household and family activities, and participation in voluntary work. For groups of people it may mean working together as partners, perhaps in a cooperative enterprise."

To hasten the rise of ownwork, Robertson would introduce "an unconditional Guaranteed Basic Income," which he'd pay for partly through the income tax, partly by abolishing most entitlements and partly by a sales tax on non-essential products and services.

Future Work lays out the advantages and implications of ownwork in admirable detail. A "new work ethic" is said to be emerging, parallel to the rise of ownwork. A "new economic theory" is emerging as well. Labor relations, the money system, the political process—all will be transformed utterly.

Unlike some post-liberal books, *Future Work* was written with the "real world" firmly in mind. Robertson virtually gets down on his knees to beg the labor leadership to see a rise of ownwork as a promise, not a threat. And he constantly addresses the concerns of mainstream economists. For example, he argues (persuasively!) that the *only* way we can combine an "internationally competitive economy" with a decent safety net is by expanding the ownwork sector of the economy.

Not to diminish Robertson's *crucial* achievements, but there are two major flaws in the book. One is the guaranteed income proposal. The guaranteed income proposal is a nonstarter in North America. It should be replaced, in future editions *and* in our movement, by a more capitalistic share-the-wealth scheme, such as a universal stock ownership plan. Second, Robertson's political strategy is pure applesauce. He writes, "The new work order will not be brought in by mass action, [but] but growing numbers of people find[ing] new ways of organizing work for themselves." Would that it were so!

John Vasconcellos:

THE ROUTE OF PEACE

Often times we never find our way out—of a bad situation—because we haven't bothered to get ourselves clear regarding how we have locked ourselves into it—with no real hope of ever getting ourselves out.

So it is with our current armed world, and our efforts at arms control, we ask, "How do we prevent war?" Our common answer, flawed fundamentally, is our almost singular focus on the questions, "Who has how many bombs, who has the advantage?" We even use 'balance of power' and 'mutually assured destruction' to indicate how well we're doing.

This sort of balance sheet logic gives the illusion we're addressing the issue, and is appealing. Yet it leads only to a never-ending, always-escalating arms competition. That's because it proceeds from an implicit negative foundational assumption regarding our own innate fearsomeness—that we human beings are innately inclined toward war; the most we can hope for and strategize is to prevent ourselves from realizing our warring destiny.

That assumption can breed only fear, leading to a paranoid and puerile flexing of muscles and counting of bombs. It becomes impossible to turn back, for it's impossible ever to satisfy our fears. Our assumption necessarily becomes a self-fulfilling, self-defeating prophecy—of more war.

We must reevaluate that assumption, if we are to develop any real hope for a peaceful world. For before our world policy comes our world vision—more precisely, our vision of ourselves

70   PERSONAL

as human beings—which informs our expectations and then our choices of behaviors.

If we truly want a way out, let our assumption no longer be implicit, let it be no longer negative. It is only the contrary faithful assumption—that we human beings are "innately inclined toward becoming constructive, life-affirming, responsible and trustworthy" (the words of Carl Rogers)—which offers a truly hopeful basis for effective peace-making policy. We can best prevent war by trusting in our peace-ability—truly, "the route for peace"!

So we begin our search for a way out by adopting such a faithful vision of ourselves, and thereby (since they share our common human nature) of all other human beings. Then we can more readily discern the means—according to our vision— that will truly enable us to move ourselves toward realizing our human peace-ability.

So let us take a road less traveled. With our newfound faithful vision, let us recognize that our involvement with another country is a relationship. And the same rules apply in every human relationship—from the most intimate to the most international; the rules of suspicion, rejection, exclusion and armaments, or the rules of trust, invitation, inclusion, and open arms.

Hopefully then our actions will proceed from our expectations, which will proceed from our faithful vision of our human nature—and will lead us toward making friends, and toward realizing our peace-ability.

Regional Ways Out

Andrea Ayvazian:

THE HONEST TRUTH

A representative democracy depends on citizens becoming informed about the issues and being able to make intelligent judgments about foreign and domestic policies. "Disinformation" generated by the government erodes a basic tenet upon which our nation is built. One way to deal with the problem of disinformation coming out of government offices and being printed as truth (and in the mainstream press it's the sole version of truth) would be to develop TRUTH SQUADS. They would be housed in every major American city and their funding and staff would be totally independent from the government. They would publish their version of truth every time a major story broke.

The TRUTH SQUADS would act as independent news bureaus and would cover both national and world affairs. (In a "free" nation, this is precisely what the media is supposed to be doing for its citizens. However, the American press rarely raises an opposing voice to the version of stories which come from Washington.) TRUTH SQUADS would have domestic offices and foreign correspondents around the world—just as the mainstream press does—and their simple, but difficult, job would be to investigate the *honest truth,* and tell it.

Diana Francis:

RAZING THE WALLS OF LANGUAGE

I t would be a major step forward if we renounce the use of all jargon and specialist vocabulary—scientific, military, political, religious, and sociological—and agree that in all instances ordinary, everyday, preferably concrete, words should be used to describe or discuss the things planned and done in the world.

That way we could no longer hide from ourselves and each other, could no longer have hidden *from* us the true human costs of policies concocted in high places and ruminated upon in stuffy buildings and in tedious meetings. A "megadeath" would be understood to be the mutilation and killing of many thousands of individual laughing, crying human beings. "Underdevelopment" would be seen as the state in which other members of the human family are forced to live in squalid shacks, without clean water, heating, lighting, or adequate food.

The other advantage of this move to plain vocabulary would be that we no longer would build walls around ourselves and the beliefs that are dear to us (beliefs from which other people might gain some benefit, if only they were not so shrouded in mystery and the often repellent language of ideology and religion). We might even present ourselves the challenge of always attempting to find new ways of expressing old truths—new ways in which to say things. This could have the benefit of making us check out, or rethink, the truth and meaning of what we are saying, and ask ourselves whether it can communicate anything real to a first-time bearer. It could provide us with the occasion to re-examine our own beliefs and commitments and open us to the insights of others.

Language is so often used to keep people apart. Let us use it instead to remind us of our common humanity.

Herb Foster:

ON THE NEED FOR A
NON-ELECTORAL PARTY

It seems obvious that the governments of the world are dysfunctional except with respect to their own narrow interests, which do not seem to include the future. Yet we continue to look to these bodies for our salvation, and to expend our energies in seeking to gain control of them.

The infrastructure is in place to serve as the basis for the development of a humane world order, but such an evolution cannot occur until the thousands of renascence groups throughout the world reject the present destructive political and economic order and move to create the structures and inter-connections which would build a new social order of compassion and creativity. Our energies cannot be freed-up for creative tasks as long as they are absorbed and squandered in the effort to function as part of the political establishment.

That the basis for such an order exists, I have no doubt. There are over seventy bio-regional groups in the U.S. alone, groups dedicated to restoring and conserving regional areas. The capacity for generosity and creativity that is manifest in the world today is literally astounding when one looks away from the tragedies surrounding us.

The possibility of achieving the kind of change necessary to avoid a total environmental collapse and a worldwide disintegration of social and political conditions is no longer open through the usual routes of political participation. Therefore, I think we should consider a *non-electoral party*. Gandhi proposed something like this before his death in 1948. He wanted the Congress party of India to withdraw entirely from politics and "dedicate itself to constructive social service" which meant the reconstruction of society by direct means.

This says that we must deliberately recast our conception of political authority and locate it where it should be—*with local, self-dependent communities*—and withdraw the mantle of authority from those who presume it on the basis of electoral performance.

If we were able to do this, we would see the role of officeholders as servants of the community. This, in turn, would free us from the debilitating and fruitless activity of contending for office and allow us to devote these precious energies to the complex task of defining the service to be performed by officeholders and to instigate the broad social support needed to enable them to become genuinely responsible to the community.

If the genius of the new-society movement is its multifarious autonomy—indeed, its anarchy (the rejection of extraneous authority, not the rejection of order)—then it seems we should reject authority in the political sphere as well, and the desire for power in that sphere. We would also, of course, reject authoritarian, hierarchical relationships within the movement!

In this view, a party, whether or not it has electoral ambitions, is essentially a grouping of people around certain basic principles which express not only tactical objectives, but philosophical and ultimately spiritual conditions of being. The new social order we seek will not emerge from the institutions which now dominate the world with tragic and destructive results, but from actions based on spiritual values suggested by Gandhi, the Greens and others, and whose development will progressively withdraw support from the old political patterns.

Dietrich Fischer:

A TEST FOR PRESIDENTS

Before we allow teenagers to drive a car, we require that they take driving lessons and pass a test. This is elementary prudence. Otherwise they could kill someone.

But the U.S. President, as military commander-in-chief, could kill tens of millions of people, possibly even wipe out the human race if he made a mistake in international affairs that led to a nuclear war. Yet we do not require that he pass any test. Where is the logic?

Of course, one could argue that being elected through a popular vote is a kind of test. But this is more a popularity contest than a test of real skills required to guide a fragile ship of state through the hidden reefs of nuclear disaster. Imagine a group of air travellers choosing one of their peers by saying, "He is the nicest guy, let him be our pilot." This would be a prescription for disaster. We demand that anyone piloting a plane go through the required training to perform that job safely. Similarly, we demand that a surgeon go through medical school and pass the necessary exams before we have confidence in her. Good intentions alone are not sufficient. We would not even allow our own mother to do heart surgery on us, even though we have no doubt that she wishes us well. Of course, we would not want to choose a president simply on the basis of having scored high on some test. We want to see and hear the person, and choose only someone in whom we have trust.

Similarly, we will want to reserve the right to choose our surgeon. But we will want to limit the choice to those who have received the necessary training and proved that they have learned the required skills. Therefore, I propose that anyone who wants to become a candidate for president receive extensive training in resolving difficult and complex conflict situations, in as realistic settings as possible. They should have to take a test to show whether they have understood whatever limited knowledge we have in defusing escalatory conflict processes. Only those who can save the world from nuclear holocaust should be entitled to be nominated as candidates for election. This should apply to all chiefs of state, at least those with control over nuclear weapons. A simple pledge to defend the Constitution is not enough. Would we issue a driver's license to someone on the basis of a solemn pledge that he or she would drive skillfully and carefully?

Diana Francis:

ON THE CARE OF
EMINENT PERSONS

Reading the report of the Commonwealth Eminent Person's Group, entitled "Mission to South Africa," I have been struck by the evidence, both in the writing and in the photographs, of the unity and fellowship forged among these powerful and distinctive individuals from such very different political, cultural, and geographical backgrounds—a unity forged by a shared purpose and a shared experience: one which evidently moved them all—a time of learning and growing together.

Thinking of that, my imagination runs on . . . How would it

be if other "eminent persons," world leaders who normally regard each other at best as opponents or competitors, at worst as enemies, could come together in some joint task or experience which is quite apart from their usual antagonisms and areas of interaction and in which they could experience their common humanity? The meeting could take the form of a work camp where they engaged together in some form of physical service for the poor. It could take the form of an art course, where they were able to explore their own creativity, a side of their personality which is perhaps often suppressed. It could take the form of a retreat in some non-partisan community, such as the Community of the Ark—a time for spiritual reflection and sharing. It could even take the form of a simple holiday in the mountains.

Not only would the experience of such a time of human encounter be a transforming one; the decision to be open to it would in itself mark a major step forward—a step out of the prison of antagonism and into the freedom of human understanding.

Gene Knudsen-Hoffman:

COUNCILS FOR NONVIOLENT SOLUTIONS

If we Americans formed ourselves into groups called Councils for Nonviolent Solutions, we could develop new and viable alternatives to offer our representatives. I see councils as a necessity for a self-governing nation.

To create such councils we would need to decide that the responsibilities of citizenship demand new efforts from us and that we must create new policies and present them to the public if we hope to change our government's actions. This gives people an opportunity to consider alternatives and make informed choices.

Councils would be composed of people (and not only professional peace people!) who meet regularly to create new policies—and who could meet rapidly whenever there's a national emergency. These could be regional councils, town councils, block councils—or just councils of concerned people anywhere.

After brainstorming, the deliberations, the hammering-out, after a new and nonviolent proposal has been created, the council spokespersons go into action.

Armed with proposals, they would seek to meet with government people, to be sure; and, perhaps even *more* important, with media people. The spokespersons would present their nonviolent bid and ask that it be televised, aired, or published. Nonviolent spokespersons (with alternatives) should be in public view whenever any critical issue is discussed.

I've been wondering if we haven't been asking far too much of our government when we write, protest, picket, and perform civil disobedience *just* to say "no" to what they're doing. Our government is not nonviolent nor is it elected by nonviolent people. So shouldn't we drop our false expectations and offer our understanding and concern for our representatives' near-impossible tasks? Could it be that our *real* work is to develop alternatives and educate our countrypeople? Milton Mayer once wrote that the American citizen was the highest official in the American government. Perhaps it's time for us to don the mantle of office and get down to the business of governing.

Richard Deats:

THE CREATIVE MOMENT
IN THE PHILIPPINES

In 1984, two years before the ouster of Ferdinand Marcos, the Little Sisters of Jesus (a community of Roman Catholic nuns) and Father José Blanco (a Filipino Jesuit priest) invited Jean and Hildegard Goss-Mayr of the International Fellowship of Reconciliation to come to the Philippines to lead workshops in active nonviolence and to meet with a wide variety of activists across the country.

The Goss-Mayrs met with clergy and laypeople to explore the nature and practice of nonviolence. Out of this developed a constituency of committed people—bishops, priests, nuns, and laypeople—who prepared for the creative moment. They formed a Philippine branch of the Fellowship of Reconciliation, known as AKKAPKA, an acronymn for Actions for Peace and Justice. In Tagalog language, *akkapka* means "I embrace you." AKKAPKA launched ongoing workshops; base communities developed which centered on active nonviolence. Corazon Aquino was part of this movement.

In tracing this astonishing development, we must return to the time when Mrs. Aquino's husband, Ninoy, offered a powerful political challenge to Marcos and was imprisoned by Marcos for seven years. During his imprisonment, Ninoy changed from a rather traditional politician to a deeply spiritual person. He studied Gandhi and came to feel that nonviolence would bring about transformation in the Philippines. Cory shared his spiritual pilgrimage. Soon after Ninoy was released from prison, he went to the United States for medical treatment. Upon his return to Manila, he was assassinated.

When Cory Aquino ran for the presidency of the Philippines, she was determined to have a nonviolent campaign. She refused to sanction violence or retaliation in response to Marcos's violence. She sought instead to develop the courage of the people, to enable them to stand up to the power of the state. She called upon people to mobilize their forces of faith to bring about their own liberation.

The nonviolent forces grew. Agapito "Butz" Aquino is Cory Aquino's brother-in-law. He attended the seminars of the Goss-Mayrs. When the military leaders, Enrile and Ramos, defected, Butz heard Cardinal Sin's radio appeal to support them nonviolently and was prepared to join them.

Despite Marcos's standing army of 300,000, Butz's plan was to meet with Enrile and Ramos. He announced over a Catholic station, Radio Veritas, that all nonviolent resisters to Marcos should meet at 11:00 P.M. at the Isatan department store to march together to the defectors' camp.

At 11:00 only six people showed up. Later, he laughed and said, "How do you have a revolution with only six people? Even Jesus Christ had twelve!" By 2:00 P.M. the next day, there were 250,000 people outside the military camp.

It was only then that the military paid attention to them. General Lim of the Marcos forces told Butz the crowd was going to be dispersed by troops.

Butz's response was: "General, we don't enjoy being here, but we're here to protect your comrades. We do not want bloodshed."

Soon a column of tanks rolled into the area. Butz jumped onto a tank; the commander inside told him to get down. Butz held on and replied, "We've been struggling for freedom for years; if it is necessary to die, we will die." Butz then got off the tank and a nun sat in the road in front of the tank. He sat beside her.

The tank began to move. The nun didn't budge, so he couldn't either. "You know my Filipino macho-mentality couldn't let that nun prove herself braver than I was." So they sat and waited.

The tank did not move again. Thousands of people moved in amongst the tanks. They held rosaries and madonnas; they gave gifts to the men in the tanks—bread, cigarettes, flowers. The men didn't know how to deal with it. Then the people cheered the soldiers, acknowledging their connectedness.

At last General Lim ordered the tanks back to the parking lot. And the people followed them, singing, offering more gifts, and tying yellow ribbons on the guns.

Later, when Butz was interviewed, he said that for a year he had been preaching active nonviolence as taught him by his brother Ninoy and Jean and Hildegard Goss-Mayr. This was his first time to practice it in a life-and-death situation. He did, and thousands of Filipinos did, and it opened the way for a nonviolent revolution that surprised the world.

Claudette Gagnon:

WAYS TO CONVERT OUR WAR-BASED ECONOMY TO A PEACE-BASED ECONOMY

Most people I know are good citizens who hate war and would vote for peace if voting for peace was all it took to bring it into being. But, these good citizens get frightened at the thought of anything new—any change. They cannot see that change might just be better for them in all ways, including their pocketbooks. Here are examples of possible conversions to a peace economy for these timid, but peace-loving people.

1. LIMESTONE AIRBASE AND ALL SUCH BASES: These bases can be converted—some bases to year-round physical-fitness camps for boys and girls, for adults and the elderly, as well as those with special needs. Convert some bases into communities where the mentally ill could live as a first step into "normal" communities as well as permanent communities for those who may never adjust. Reduce prison overcrowding by using bases for prison population.

2. BATH IRONWORKS AND SIMILAR MANUFACTURERS: Use these facilities to build submarines for aquaculture, to build ships to be mother ships for the aqua subs, and to build recreational ships for people.

3. PLANTS THAT MAKE MISSILES FOR NUCLEAR WARHEADS: These plants could build space labs and space shuttles, and space ships for deep-space study.

4. PLANTS THAT MAKE GUNS: We can convert these plants so they can start rebuilding the rail system of the U.S.; make underwater exploration equipment; make carpentry, farming, and kitchen tools; and make new machine tooling.

5. COMPANIES THAT MAKE CHEMICAL AND NUCLEAR MATERIALS USED FOR WAR PURPOSES: There are many medical possibilities in both cure and prevention with chemicals and, yes, even nuclear materials. Research can go into solving the nuclear-waste-disposal problem; to clean up the chemical mess prevalent all over this planet; to clean the air and water and to keep these clean; to find equipment and methods of fighting fires; to find new methods of trash disposal.

6. MAINE MARITIME ACADEMY AND ALL SUCH ACADEMIES: These could be converted into a college to study aquaculture and other related fields. Convert the Air Force Academy to a study center on airplane designs, and deep-space travel. The Coast Guard Academy and the Coast Guard itself could stay as is. Its emphasis should be ocean rescue.

7. ARMY, NAVY, MARINE, AIRFORCE PERSONNEL: The officers have managerial skills. The converted bases and plants would need their leadership capabilities. The engineers and officers with scientific skills could be used to help build new and

repair old roads, bridges, rail systems, hospitals, *ad-infinitum*. The soldiers could have construction jobs on the roads, bridges, rail systems, landscaping, etc.

The conversion of any army base, shipbuilding plant, or missile plant creates jobs while the conversion is going on and jobs after the conversion is completed. Businesses which now thrive on these installations would keep their businesses going while the conversion was taking place by servicing the people doing the renovations. When renovations are completed the "new" base or plant would need the services of these same businesses.

In the first paragraph I said that a change from a war economy into a peace economy might be beneficial to the pocketbooks of people. Our country spends a very large percentage of our income on war products. For the most part these war products cannot be eaten or used for anything but destruction. Just think how productive the above suggestions are!

The ideas presented here are not to be accomplished in one fell swoop! They could be worked on at one army base or one missile plant at a time. The knowledge gained from the first successes would gain momentum and other installations would follow.

Mark Shepard:

INDIA: JUSTICE THAT UNITES

The true practice of law is to unite parties riven asunder.
—GANDHI

W hat would a court system look like that served the people instead of rulers and lawyers? One answer comes from a Gandhian worker in India named Harivallabh

Parikh. He calls it the Peoples' Court and it handles anything from a marital dispute to murder.

Harivallabh tells how it started. As a young man he took part in India's struggle for independence; he trained in village development work at Gandhi's ashram. After independence in 1947 he decided to find a village in which to settle. He went to eastern Gujarat state, to a mostly tribal region, and began walking through the villages.

After many days he stopped at one village to restock his supplies. He bought some corn and sat under a tree to grind it into flour. The tribal people (Adivasis) thought it strange to see a man grinding—grinding was woman's work! So Harivallabh soon had a crowd to talk to.

From these few villagers, Harivallabh soon found out that the village was plagued by disputes; most of them were over minor matters, but they often ended in killing. Since the villagers invited him to settle there, Harivallabh accepted and brought his wife and a few belongings. Soon he convinced some of the villagers to let him help try to settle their disputes. It was from these beginnings that the Peoples' Court grew.

Over three decades later, Harivallabh is overseeing the development of 1,100 tribal villages, containing 1.5 million people. Economic and social gains have been remarkable, but the heart of the program is still the People's Court. It is without legal sanction in the eyes of the state, but the government does not interfere with it any longer.

Complaints are taken at any time by the Secretary of the Court, who then issues summons. The villagers almost always respect these summons—mainly because the community expects them to. In fact, it is often the guilty party who brings the case to the Peoples' Court!

If a villager ignores the summons, fifty or a hundred villagers may call on the person to attend. If he doesn't, five hundred might go to visit him. If that doesn't work, villagers might fast in front of the person's house. Eventually the person attends.

The Court usually meets once or twice a month and handles a number of cases at each session. When a case comes up, each side tells its story, while Harivallabh asks questions. Other witnesses are called. Then Harivallabh states how he understands the case, to check if he's gotten it straight. If the case is fairly simple, he then gives a judgment. Harder cases are decided by a jury selected from friends of each side. Harivallabh steps in only if the jury can't reach a decision.

The judgment is written out by Harivallabh, and signed or thumb-printed by both sides. Here are some sample cases:

A childless widow's house and land have been occupied by her in-laws, leaving her without property of her own. (This is an Adivasi custom.) The Court tells the in-laws to return the land to the widow.

A villager complains that his married daughter has been at his house getting over an illness; but the husband has refused to pay for the girl's food and medical costs. The judgment: The husband must bring his wife home and pay the medical bills. The father bears the cost of food she ate in his house.

Harivallabh tells of one murder case. Two men named Fatu and Ramji quarrelled over a pair of chickens Ramji had borrowed and never replaced. The argument ended with Fatu shooting Ramji with an arrow and killing him. Fatu rushed to Harivallabh and told him what he had done.

The case was brought to the People's court. The judgment was that Fatu should farm Ramji's land in place of his victim, until Ramji's son was old enough to take over. Also, Fatu had to eat with Ramji's family once a week.

At first Ramji's family and Fatu resisted eating together. Fatu was served his meals outside the door. But in time Fatu was welcomed inside. Ramji "paid his dues," and he and the family were reconciled.

The Peoples' Court is a means of social education. From the Court the Adivasis learn new standards of conduct, fair play, and justice. They learn to respond to the moral will of their community. In the village councils they learn they can handle their own disputes and offenses—that they don't have to rely on government structures that they have little part in.

And they respect their own processes.

Mark Shepard:

SHANTI SENA: INDIA'S PEACE BRIGADE

Riots are a major plague in India. Most have occurred between Hindus and Moslems; the worst of them over the last three decades took the lives of over a thousand people in a single city.

In 1922, Gandhi suggested the idea of a nonviolent civilian peacekeeping force (Shanti Sena) to deal with riots. The idea failed to take hold during his lifetime.

Today, the standard bearer of Gandhi's vision is Narayan Desai who lives and teaches in Vedcchi, Gujarat, and was a student of Gandhi.

Narayan Desai describes how Shanti Sena works: The first step is to announce that *shanti sainiks* ("peace soldiers") will work in the riot area. At the same time it issues a statement about issues involved in the riot. The statement does not place blame on either side, but calls insead for an end to the violence. Over the next few days, the shanti sainiks arrive in the city by train. They are mostly part-time volunteers usually active in India's Sarvodaya, or peace movement. And they are mostly Hindu—an important factor when trying to discourage a Hindu majority from violence against Moslems!

When the sainiks arrive, they form themselves into small groups and try to meet once a day. Decisions are made by concensus; between meetings, they are made by a chosen leader.

Some of the sainiks contact local officials and civic leaders to enlist their cooperation. Sometimes the people contacted are willing to call publicly for an end to the violence or meet with leaders of the opposition.

Most sainik groups patrol areas of the city where violence is likely. The patrols talk to people on the street, or even go from door to door. They find out what is on the people's minds and talk of the need for peace. The patrols discourage violence by persuasion and by their friendly presence.

But they are ready if violence breaks out. They are prepared to rush directly betweeen the attacking sides, shouting peace slogans as they absorb blows from both sides. Women take part as well as men. (The rioters are less likely to hit women.)

One group of sainiks may take the special job of quelling rumors. Very often one side will attack the other in response to a false story from troublemakers, the media, the government, or word of mouth. "Shanti Sena fights rumors with facts," says Desai. When a rumor is heard, the sainiks go to the scene of the reported incident and check out the story so they can tell people the truth. The facts are spread by word of mouth, daily bulletins, notices on wallboards, and sometimes by radio.

Sometimes sainiks will live among people who are frightened. Other times they will live among people they are supposed to fear. One of the ways the sainiks combat fear is by organizing silent processions. Sainiks and people from the conflicting sides walk together silently through areas that have suffered from rioting. In Calcutta three hundred people marched in such a procession. All along the way, the closed shops reopened as the marchers passed.

Once the violence subsides, the sainiks work to ease the suffering the riots have caused. They organize medical relief, pass out food and clothing, help build new homes, perform sanitation work, and remove bodies.

Finally comes the work of reconciling the opposing communities. In one city, Hindu leaders were persuaded to visit Moslem refugee camps to invite the Moslems to return to their homes and to personally guarantee the Moslems' safety. In another, Hindus were convinced to give money to rebuild Moslem homes they had destroyed only a week earlier.

Before sainiks leave a riot-struck city, they usually try to organize a peace committee, made up of citizens from both sides of the conflict. The job of this committee is to keep an eye on relations between the communities and to try to diffuse tension if it arises. One hopes these committees can evolve to prevention of riots.

Besides combatting riots, Shanti Sena does relief work after natural disasters—floods, famines, and earthquakes. They try to organize people to help themselves instead of waiting for help from the outside.

Gandhi once said, "We are constantly astonished at the amazing discoveries in the field of violence. But I maintain that far more undreamt of and seemingly impossible discoveries will be made in the field of nonviolence."

Shanti Sena seems to be one of these discoveries.

Don Moseley:

WALK IN PEACE

On the 25th of February, 1987, the WALK IN PEACE campaign, initiated by the staff at Jubilee Partners of Comer, Georgia, was launched in Washington, D.C., with a press conference and a series of meetings with Congressional members and staff. The main goal of this campaign is to help rehabilitate every amputee in Nicaragua. They also intend to help build support for diplomatic initiatives in the region, such as the Contadora process, instead of the military approach.

On October 20, 1986, a tour group of reporters and religious leaders organized by Jubilee Partners was in a plane on the way to Nicaragua when a road mine exploded near the village of

Pantasma, Jinotega, in north-central Nicaragua. Six people were either killed instantly or died while waiting for medical help. About forty others were injured, including twelve who lost one or both of their legs. Some of the Jubilee delegation visited the amputees, and all of them were deeply moved by the tragedy.

The scene that haunted them most was Elda Sanchez, a little girl just seven years old, with one leg blown off and the other shattered in so many places that it may never be fully normal again. Elda was in critical condition for days, but she survived. So did her father, Amancio Sanchez (who also lost one leg), and her beautiful nineteen-year-old aunt, Carmen (who lost both legs).

Jimmy Carter helped them obtain visas, and Jubilee made arrangements for them to come to the U.S. the next spring to be fitted with artificial legs. They were escorted from Managua to Jubilee by a Witness for Peace delegation and returned to Managua the same way.

A doctor on the staff of Emory University's Center for Rehabilitation Medicine agreed to donate his services and to keep other expenses as low as possible. (The medical care was still very expensive.) Thus, three wounded Nicaraguan civilians were helped.

The most reliable estimates from Nicaraguan medical authorities seem to be that there are some two thousand amputees (from all causes) now in Nicaragua, and nearly one third lost their legs during the past year—mostly due to the war, of course.

Jubilee Partners hopes to supplement the work of the Red Cross in Nicaragua, which can produce artificial legs for only about two hundred people each year.

But Jubilee Partners doesn't stop at aid to the suffering Nicaraguans. There are deaths, injuries, and sufferings on both sides of the battle lines, and many contra soldiers are hardly more than boys themselves. "We are exploring ways for WALK IN PEACE to help rehabilitate their amputees as well. There will have to be special arrangements made for their medical care and mutually acceptable ways to oversee the process and to verify that funds are used appropriately."

Greg Guma:

FREEDOM OF AMPLIFIED SPEECH

Media in the United States primarily are privately owned businesses, but their main functions are public. That even includes entertainment programming, which is supposedly based on public desires. Why, then, should these "public forums" not be available to all sorts of people, as long as public access doesn't prevent media businesses from performing their other functions?

This idea is in line with the First Amendment. Nothing in the Bill of Rights prevents Congress from taking affirmative steps to help people obtain access to public forums—including their local newspapers and TV stations. It's not a question of giving "listeners" special rights. Rather, it would be both fair and perfectly legal to make sure that free speech isn't snuffed out because the people who own the media decide they want to share it only with big corporations and politicians.

What does access really mean? Certainly not only the right to make political speeches and buy commercial time or advertising space. All sorts of messages are valid; each of us has something to say and the basic right to say it. On the other hand, editors have a right to establish "time, place, and manner" rules. It is only practical to set reasonable limits on the length of the messages, when they appear, or how many times they can be repeated.

In the U.S., we don't want to stop journalists from searching for and printing the truth. But when the newspaper, radio station, or TV channel is the only effective way to get an idea or an opinion across, it's only fair that these resources be shared by as many people as possible. This might be called freedom of amplified speech. It is completely consistent with the original intentions of the First Amendment, merely adding new media to the list.

In practical terms, freedom of amplified speech would mean expanding people's access to newspapers. At the moment, corporations have virtually unlimited access; much of the news is generated by the source. Access for average people would allow journalists to remain "informed speakers" but would open up the medium to others (and not only on the letter page). In the end, this would help the press to improve its work of keeping an eye on abuses of power.

TV and radio would be affected more significantly, since most broadcasters aren't open to non-professionals. Access would mean that, as Andy Warhol put it, "everyone will be a star for fifteen minutes." Reasonable limits could be set, applied equally to the rich and poor, to those whose views agree with station owners and those whose ideas they oppose. In the cable-TV industry, access would clearly mean making a channel and necessary equipment available. Though some people would be more articulate and technically knowledgeable than others, experience would tend to reduce the differences over time.

These new rights should apply to individuals, not to institutions. The idea is that freedom of speech is a personal right and that freedom of the press really means the right to use various media without prior censorship. The First Amendment says nothing about the freedom of businesses to spread their views. They aren't prohibited from doing so, of course, but they're not protected under the Constitution.

Using autonomy as a key value, we should fight for the rights originally granted by the First Amendment. Certainly, we should avoid government control of communication (which is proceeding rapidly under the rationale of national security). But what mainly threatens free speech today is not government action but control of society by enormous economic interests, which want to determine what we think as well as what we buy. The solution is strong action to recreate a free marketplace of ideas.

We cannot manage our own lives and control our society if we lack the sense of dignity which comes from free self-expression. Democracy cannot be manufactured by either the press or the government. The best these institutions can do is maintain an open environment. If that is done, the cultivation of vast human potential can provide a foundation for the development of a truly self-governing society.

Mark Satin:

SELF-RELIANCE GOES MAINSTREAM

S t. Paul, Minnesota, has become the first city to adopt a "self-reliant local development" strategy. For the past two and a half years, David Morris and his Institute for Local Self-Reliance (ILSR) have been working out of the St. Paul mayor's office to develop and implement the Homegrown Economy project. Recently the mayor's office released the first public report on the project, a glossy twenty-eight-page booklet, and announced the beginnings of a three-month publicity campaign.

"A self-reliant city is a coherent, integrated city," ILSR president David Morris told us after a busy day at the mayor's office. "St. Paul is trying to look at its city as a living organism whose parts are interconnected. No other city that I know of is [trying to do that]."

Morris has practically moved to St. Paul on a semi-permanent basis, despite the fact that ILSR is located in Washington, D.C. "[One of my functions] here is to engage all sectors of the community in a conversation," he says. "I meet with third grade teachers to tell them how to encourage invention, how to develop invention workshops in the public schools. I meet with community organizations to discuss the concept of a neighborhood-based service delivery system."

Morris's job isn't the easiest in the world. "[People's] initial response to the term 'self-reliance' is a warm one," he says. "But when it's then defined as 'meeting as much as possible of your human and material needs from within your boundaries,' people become a little skeptical."

St. Paul Mayor George Latimer not only enthusiastically supports Morris's work, he also understands it. "Most mayors are project-oriented," he has been quoted as saying, "and although the Homegrown Economy can be demonstrated in projects, finally it is not a project. It is a process, a way that people look at things."

But the Homegrown Economy is *also* "projects," and quite a few of them have just been launched or are about to be launched. There is now, for example, an *incubator facility* (i.e., a big old warehouse) that the city rents to fledgling small businesses at very low cost. There is a *trade center* that acts as a link between small businesses and the global economy.

A *block nurse program* run by registered nurses and volunteers is able to keep elderly people out of nursing homes (and cut their costs by 300 percent to 500 percent!). A program to turn *old tires* into pothole fill is on the drawing boards, as is a program that would purchase *wood chips* to substitute for coal (Minneapolis-St. Paul disposes of 40,000 tons a year of diseased elm trees).

St. Paul is by no means ILSR's only current project. Earlier this year, Philadelphia embraced a multi-million-dollar solid waste management strategy that was developed largely by ILSR. "Since 1974," Morris told us proudly, "through our staff and a network of experts, the Institute has been a technical adviser to [dozens of] cities, states, businesses, and neighborhood organizations."

In truth, ILSR has evolved considerably since 1974. Its

founders envisioned not only self-reliant cities, but self-reliant and self-governing *neighborhoods*. ("I foresee the creation of elected neighborhood governments," Morris told *Mother Earth News* in 1974, when he was still in his twenties.) This year ILSR may get $50,000 from its work in Philadelphia alone, but in the mid-1970s it was trying to keep itself afloat selling T-shirts celebrating the comet Kahoutek.

We asked Morris how he'd been drawn to the self-reliance concept, and he told us about the time in the late 1960s when he'd moved to Chile and set up a news service (and eventually wrote a book about Allende's government). "When I was in Chile, I realized I was living in a country that was the size of New York City! [Unlike New York,] it owned hardly any of its resources or industry. And yet—it was going through a peaceful, democratic change.

"At roughly the same time, New York City was declaring itself bankrupt. It said it was bankrupt economically—I'd say it was also bankrupt morally. It was infinitely richer than Chile but it declared it didn't have the resources to deal with its problems!

"The contrast between the two led me to the idea of the self-reliant city. I have to be candid and say that [at first] we were not accorded a great welcome. But the technologies [making urban self-reliance feasible] have progressed, and some of the kinds of people who were not interested in—or sympathetic to—cities fifteen years ago, are now mayors and city councilpeople and heads of administrative agencies."

Harold Willens:

WHAT IS THE ULTIMATE CORPORATE RESPONSIBILITY?

The opposition to the nuclear arms race has nothing to do with politics. It has everything to do with common sense—the common sense to see through a system where no one is in control except a self-perpetuating myth that says the more missiles you have, the safer you are.

Yet, the nuclear weapons issue generates surprisingly little furor in the United States. Nothing moves us to outrage.

Indignation, perhaps, but certainly not outrage. If we are to survive, however, we must act.

Business is the most flexible and change-oriented segment of our society. Successful business leaders stand ready to abandon unworkable policies and adopt new strategies to meet new challenges. The capabilities and characteristics that make for success in the competitive marketplace are precisely those that can break the momentum of the arms race.

Excessive military spending is not a prescription for prosperity, rather it contributes directly to our economic woes. It bears directly on the major aspects of the economic problems that continue to plague us: foreign competition, low productivity, and, because innovative brains are often drained away from business by the military complex, slow technological progress in our general business economy.

In contrast to consumer and producer goods, military goods neither add directly to the present standard of living nor increase productivity of the economic system. Dollars spent on weapons, tanks, fighter planes, and submarines are dead-end dollars. They consume enormous quantities of valuable resources but put nothing back into the economic system.

Military spending may, in the short term, stimulate employment and purchasing power, but in the long run it drains the economy.

It is time for business leaders to lead the American people in asking whether the safety of their streets and neighborhoods, the quality of their schools, and the security of their jobs are not real aspects of national security that should be weighed against the illusion of safety produced by an absurdly excessive quantity of nuclear weapons.

Without a sense that there is a future in which we can see ourselves learning, growing, achieving, and procreating, we will find ourselves slowly losing our will to survive. There are compelling reasons why the United States should seize the initiative in calling a halt to a form of competition that reduces our security and does deep damage to our economy.

The following step-by-step program of American initiatives would represent a methodical process for breaking the momentum of the nuclear arms race. In each step, our country could take independent action that would demonstrate good faith and give the Soviets an opportunity to demonstrate theirs as well.

1. The United States would suspend all further testing of nuclear weapons and challenge the Soviet Union to do the same while we meet to conclude negotiation of a comprehensive test-ban treaty. If the Soviets continued to test, or refused to conclude the treaty within a reasonable time, the U.S. would no longer be bound to this proposal.
2. We would next invoke a moratorium on the flight-testing of nuclear-weapons delivery systems. Like the ban on testing, this step would be relatively easy to verify. Depending on Soviet compliance, this moratorium would prevent the testing of new destabilizing delivery systems.
3. The U.S. would initiate yet another moratorium on the deployment of any *new* nuclear-weapons systems.
4. After taking the first three steps, we would face the far more difficult issue of banning the actual production of nuclear

warheads. We should keep in mind that the Soviet Union has formally accepted the principle of on-site inspection for arms-control verification as part of a comprehensive test ban. Similar kinds of inspection could effectively stop an entire new generation of weapons.

5. After this incremental process, we could begin to appraise existing arsenals and develop a series of measures to carry out a stable, orderly, balanced program of reductions. Each side would keep a mutually acceptable deterrent capability.

These five steps are not meant to be seen as a grand design or as the only solution, but rather as a road map—a way to get someplace. They constitute a methodical, manageable, prudent process that steers clear of both paranoia and panacea.

It is nonsense to insist that resolving the nuclear arms dilemma should be left to the experts. The experts are, after all, the ones who created the policy that brought us to the present point of potentially terminal peril. The myth of expertise is exactly that—a myth. It takes scientific skills to make a hydrogen bomb. It takes only common sense to know when there are too many.

It is my conviction that by speaking out with clarity and courage we can persuade our people and our government that—just as in any bad business deal—there is always a *way out*.

Gene Keyes:

FORCE WITHOUT FIREPOWER

Nonviolent military forces may seem a preposterous contradiction in terms, but there are in the U.S. military components with mottos such as "Alone, Unarmed,

Unafraid" (reconnaissance pilots), "That Others May Live" (air rescue), and "Strive to Save Lives" (Medevac).

A working definition of Unarmed Services would be men and women forming an entire military command without weapons; well equipped for mobility and logistics; trained to accept casualties, not inflict them. The essential duty of these unarmed services would be to give life, never to take it.

Here are ten different missions:

● RESCUE ACTION: The employment of military capability for saving lives and setting up disaster relief in times of natural or man-made catastrophe; generally in environments or conditions not manageable by local or civilian resources.

● CIVIC ACTION: The use of military forces, especially in less-developed areas, for social-service projects such as local construction, farming, public health, transportation, education, communication, conservation, community development, and the like.

● COLOSSAL ACTION: The employment of military capability, especially logistic, in constructive social enterprises of enormous magnitude, possibly requiring ships in the thousands, aircraft in the tens of thousands, personnel in hundreds of millions, and dollars in hundreds of billions per year (i.e., "We advocate that all standing armies everywhere be used for the work of essential reforestation in the countries to which they belong, and that each country shall provide expeditionary forces to cooperate in the greater tasks of land reclamation in the Sahara and other deserts." Richard St. Barbe Baker, *Green Glory*).

● FRIENDLY PERSUASION: The use or display of nonviolent military force during normal or crisis periods for such purposes as good will, deterrence, show of strength, propaganda, hostage deployment, and political, psychological, or economic warfare; by means such as goodwill visits, public and joint maneuvers, and the delivery of messages, food, equipment, gifts, or hostages, whether requested or not.

● GUERILLA ACTION: Aggressive and unconventional initiatives by irregular but disciplined unarmed forces waging a revolutionary and/or defensive struggle against a more powerful opponent. ("Only in a world moving toward disarmament could we use effectively what might be called the unarmed services of the United States . . . [including] a nonviolent freedom force that could help activate the politically suppressed in countries like Paraguay, South Africa, Albania, etc." Arthur Waskow, *Running Riot*, 1970; and *Toward the Unarmed Forces of the United States*, 1965; composite quotation.)

• POLICE ACTION: The use of unarmed military units for law enforcement, peace observation, and peacekeeping duties in situations beyond the control of local authority. (Beginning in 1964 the United Nations sent more than 7,000 peacekeeping-force soldiers to Cyprus to keep peace between Turkish and Greek Cypriots.)

• DEFENSE: The assignment of unarmed maneuver elements to close with and resist invasion troops to the death without killing them; the assignment of other unarmed land, sea, air, and civilian forces to active duty in accordance with national strategy for guarding political, cultural, and territorial integrity, public security, and civil liberty. (". . . The existence of a fearless nonviolent army, which would offer resistance to the last man, might act as a stronger warning to the potential invader than an invisible system of resistance cells." Theodor Ebnert, *Organizational Preparations for Nonviolent Civilian Defense*, 1964)

• BUFFER ACTION: The deployment of unarmed military force between belligerents before, during, or after active hostilities. ("The presence of a body of regular world guards or peace guards, intervening with no weapons whatsoever between two forces combating or about to combat, might have considerable effect." Salvador de Madariage and Jayaprakash Narayan, *Blueprint for a World Commonwealth*.)

• EXPEDITIONARY ACTION: An unarmed military mission across national boundaries with a comparatively limited objective or duration; may involve extraterritorial rather than home-soil defense action, or defense of another nation on its own territory,

100

or temporary intervention in restraint of flagrant injustice, oppression, invasion, or genocide.

● INVASION: An unarmed military campaign across national boundaries, with a comparatively long-range objective or duration, in restraint of flagrant injustice, oppression, invasion, or genocide. ("If you meet a Spanish civilian or soldier, greet him and share your food with him. If he fires on you, arm yourself with your faith and your conviction and continue your march." King Hassan II of Morocco in a message to 350,000 civilians poised to invade Spanish Sahara; *New York Times*, November 6, 1975.)

Is it too much to expect that soldiers on active defense duty could give their lives, yet not kill? I argue that the military ethos of courage in facing death is not a function of killing people. To ask whether anyone could be expected to enlist in a front-line unarmed force is to ask why any soldiers anywhere go to war, volunteer for hazardous duty, or lay down their own lives that others may live.

Deena Hurwitz:

NONVIOLENCE IN THE ISRAELI OCCUPIED TERRITORIES

Nonviolence is being taken more seriously these days in the occupied West Bank. One sign is a Palestinian Center for the Study of Nonviolence, established in January 1985 in East Jerusalem. A January 1986 demonstration near the village of Qattaneh involved Palestinians, Israelis, North Americans and Europeans.

The Israeli Land Authority had uprooted olive trees on the

terraced hillside of Qattaneh, a West Bank village approximately five kilometers northwest of Jerusalem. The trees were replanted within Israel's 1967 border. Despite documents showing the location of the land on the West Bank and proving the trees to be between twenty and sixty years old, the villagers were told the land was "state land," and therefore the trees were state property.

The Center, working with the Israeli chapter of the International Fellowship of Reconciliation, organized a tree replanting at the site, and one hundred and fifty people planted saplings in the holes from which the olive trees had been removed. Planting trees on the West Bank without permission of the military authorities is a punishable offense. Some planters were arrested; others were nonviolently surrounded by large groups of demonstrators who prevented their arrest. The demonstrators had on their side, besides moral justice, strength through numbers and publicity through television cameras and journalists.

Ultimately the demonstrators made an agreement with the military governor and the Land Authority by which the demonstrators would retreat and the trees already planted would not be touched. However, when the group returned the next day to water them, the trees were gone. They had been pulled up an hour after the demonstrators left.

Israeli television and newspapers carried extensive coverage of the incident. Two subsequent tree-planting demonstrations have been held in Qattaneh. More important, despite the familiar outcome—Palestinian property destroyed or expropriated—the demonstrations highlighted the injustice of the incident and left people feeling empowered because it was nonviolent. It was more then "just another clash between Israeli authorities and Arab violence."

It is this point that is stressed by nonviolent proponents in Israel and the occupied territories. The history of Israeli-Palestinian/Arab conflict is one of the repeated failures of militarism to arbitrate or achieve any just solutions for either people. A Palestinian state co-existing in peace with Israel, and both with their Arab neighbors, cannot be obtained by force.

Nonviolence is especially important in this region, where diplomacy seems to be faltering, people feel hopeless and powerless, and military force has proved futile.

Palestinians have been skeptical about nonviolence. Some perceive it as a threat to the authority of the PLO. Others consider it ineffectual, that questioning armed struggle must be counter-revolutionary. But nonviolent demonstrations have begun to convince some Palestinians that while it may be non-militarist, it is certainly radical in goals and means. Mubarak Awad, co-director of the Palestinian Center for the Study of Nonviolence, predicts that "if a lot of people get involved with nonviolence, the PLO cannot stay out of it."

Creating confrontations between the system and its victims, without compromising just means, may expose the system's evils without attacking the individuals who happen to work for or enforce it. By creating moral dilemmas that individuals must face, nonviolent action allows them to be human.

When Palestinians perceive Israelis as human (and vice versa—seeing them as people distinct from the structure in which they operate) they have an opportunity to judge for themselves. This way they are not forced into defensive postures and are much more apt to change.

Fear is the greatest weapon in the hands of the authorities. Central to nonviolence is the voluntary acceptance of suffering. What is most empowering is the sense of being in control of oneself and the situation. Persons motivated by the dignity rooted in the power of a just cause and the acceptance of its consequences will be beyond fear.

Rehumanizing the enemy is a singularly important task. We do not act to defeat or humiliate the opponent, but rather to win his or her friendship and understanding. Nonviolence has the power, Mubarak Awad wrote, "to remove the irrational fear of Arab violence which presently cements Israeli society."

Nonviolence requires more imagination and discipline than violence. Success through nonviolence may come more slowly, and in new and different terms. Soldiers don't suddenly refuse orders, neither do Arabs and Jews decide overnight to demonstrate together against injustice. But if a clear link is made between the goal and the means for achieving it, the peace won will be more enduring. There is no way to stop the power of a just truth.

Amos Gvirtz:

COMMENTS ON THE MIDDLE EAST CONFLICT

I do not want to examine the conflict between the Israelis and Palestinians in its historical and emotional details—who is right; why people did what they did, etc. It is more important to identify what kind of conflict this is, and what kinds of nonviolent suggestions we have for dealing with it. What are the possibilities for a nonviolent resolution?

First, the characteristics of the conflict can be generally outlined: One group of persons has entered the 'life area' of another, and pushed the latter group out in an historical process.

What do I mean by life area? I believe all people have their territory—what I call their life area. For example, in the early American history of European colonialism in North America, the Europeans invaded the life area of the native American Indian peoples. This is similar to the Middle East conflict. This is not to say that the early American conflict with the Native Americans is exactly the same as the present Middle East conflict. In North America, for example, Native Americans did not provide labor for the white colonial Europeans. In North

America, the historical process led toward a total threat to the lives and existence of the Native American population.

In the Middle East, from the very beginning, Palestinians were working for the Jews. It wasn't exactly slavery, but they worked. This interaction, even if unequal, mitigates the conflict somewhat because there is some interaction between the two groups. In North America, the conflict is notable for the total absence of such interaction. This interaction in the Middle East means that, on occasion, there is a possibility for some Jews and some Arabs to have common cause on a particular issue (such as a strike by workers). These kinds of relationships mitigate, but do not stop, the historical process that continues to push the Palestinians out of their life area.

One of the central problems to face in the Middle East conflict, therefore, is this continued historical process.

Yet, the very interaction that I mentioned—due to the large number of Palestinian workers—provides the greatest modern potential for a non-violent struggle in the Middle East. If we could imagine, for example, a general Palestinian strike—then most construction in Israel (as well as in the Occupied Territories) would come to a grinding halt. Agriculture would be crippled without pickers; garbage collection and sanitation services would stop in hospitals, factories, and public buildings, as well as in offices—one can begin to imagine the potential disruption that such a strike would cause.

Today in Israel and the Occupied Territories, there are a few groups that try to work for nonviolence. The oldest is the Israeli section of the War Resisters League, and now we have the new chapter of the International Fellowship of Reconciliation (Arabs and Jews for Nonviolence, Fellowship, and Peace), and the new Palestinian Center for the Study of Nonviolence in the West Bank (Jerusalem). As I understand the task of these groups, it is to bring nonviolent conflict 'to the people'—and prove that this method is available to them.

The task, however, is not the same for Jews as for Arabs. The Israeli Jews must be far more engaged in "preventive nonviolence" in order to prevent further confiscation and oppression of the Palestinians. The Palestinians, obviously, have the task of more active nonviolence that struggles directly against the conditions the Jews are working to prevent.

I believe we can learn from the struggle of Martin Luther King, Jr., about the possibility of cooperation between Israeli Jews and the Palestinians. For example, Palestinian use of nonviolence will reduce much of the fear on the Jewish side, and this will enable them to focus more clearly on the real issues and rights and survival of the Palestinian people. If the Palestinian struggle does not risk the very survival of the Jewish people, they will be able to focus on the issues of Palestinian survival. Common actions of Jews and Palestinians together will reduce fear and build trust for further common work and life.

My theory and my hope is that democratic nonviolent action within the Palestinian society will give more chance for peace and democracy *within* that society than will a violent campaign. We must all be aware that dictatorship is a constant result of the violent defeat of colonialism. I believe that nonviolent conflict reduces the threat to both Jew and Palestinian, and holds the most promise for peace, justice, and co-existence between our people.

Yehezkel Landau:

A LIBERATING MOVE

(Excerpt from a letter) April 8, 1987

The alternative I've been advocating, to whoever would listen, is this: an announcement by the government of Israel that it will facilitate the phased transfer of Palestinian refugees from Lebanon to the West Bank, and the construction of permanent dwellings for them with funds to be donated by private citizens and governments anywhere. Paying the bill will come later; saving lives (threatened by Al-Amal, or Syrian or Phalangist forces in Lebanon) and lifting spirits come first.

Such a liberating move would, I believe, produce a psycho-spiritual sea-change among both Palestinians and Israelis, who will be helped to see that co-existence means interdependence and taking responsibility for the survival and welfare of the other. Negotiation over sovereignty and borders, and security guarantees for both peoples, will follow—in a more conducive atmosphere. Meanwhile, the Palestinians will see that we really want them to live, and live in the same homeland together with us. And Israelis will see how military and political power can be used, for a change, in the service of life and liberation.

Joseph Abileah:

MIDDLE EAST CONFEDERATION

L ed by convictions which I acquired early in life in this country, I have been campaigning for many years for an alternative solution to the everlasting conflict between Arabs and Jews, or more particularly between Palestinians and Is-raelis. The area I have selected is the search for a political framework that would satisfy the needs of the conflicting parties. This is the pattern of a confederation that would do justice to the various territorial demands and take into consid-eration important geopolitical views which, in turn, will be the basis for economic development.

As a political alternative, the Society for Middle East Confed-eration, founded years ago, promotes proposals for a confederative union in Israel with a Palestinian state. This should obviously be joined by the Kingdom of Jordan in order to secure to this country free access to seaports and provide for a greater hinterland for development.

The first common concern of the new confederation will be the solution of the Palestinian refugee problem, which will be the common responsibility of all the member states. The problems that will arise in relation to the remaining states in the Middle East should not be underestimated. To create a federal army in order to protect the confederation should be avoided by removing causes. Syria has been engaged in expansion politics throughout recent decades. Owing to the huge underdeveloped but essentially fertile desert region, this country was obliged to oppose the cutting off of Lebanon in the forties and has not recognized so far the independence of its neighbors.

The first step, therefore, for peace in our region would be the irrigation of the Syrian dessert, which in fact was started by the construction of the dam on the Euphrates River in 1968. When I was asked about the foreign policy of a visualized confederation, I replied: "It would be dedicated to the welfare of all neighbors."

Diana Francis:

BRINGING THEM ALL BACK HOME

In our present society in Britain, young people often feel alienated from adult life; so they "drop out," exist on social security, live in bed-sits, squats, or "benders," and spend their time together hanging out. They are often shamefully treated by the police, and the adult world in general is hostile toward them because of their appearance and because they do not respect adult ways.

These youngsters often are committed to alternative values and behave—to each other especially, but often to others, too—with tolerance and compassion. But they seem aimless, or else committed only to "smashing the State," having no real ideas about what they want in its place or how they can organize for the changes they'd like to see. Sometimes they drift into drugs or petty crime and the future for them seems bleak.

I should like to start a center for such people locally, where they can obtain advice and counselling when they are in trouble; where they can work through their grievances and anger and sense of futility and come to a feeling of self-respect: a feeling that what they do and who they are *counts* and can have an effect on the world; that in them lies hope for the future. I'd like to help them find the skills to reflect their self-respect in their behavior and to discover that the sense of community they already have with each other gives them a wonderful base from which to act for change; to realize that their compassion and their rejection of materialism and arbitrary "authority" makes them the best possible people to help build a new, much better, sort of society.

Dietrich Fischer:

SELF-DETERMINATION

The British government has tried to suppress the conflict between Catholics and Protestants in Northern Ireland through military force, without success. It might be time to try another solution. A similar conflict developed in the Jura region of Switzerland between a French-speaking Catholic minority and a German-speaking Protestant majority. When petitions and demonstrations by the Catholic minority for internal autonomy failed to achieve results, acts of violence began to emerge. There were increasing instances of arson, although no lives were lost yet. But there is little doubt that if that situation had been allowed to persist, it could eventually have developed into a full-scale civil war as in Northern Ireland. In 1978, after a long delay, the government of the Canton Berne finally held a referendum in the contested region. Of six districts, the three bordering on France chose to form their own independent canton (called Jura), whereas the three districts closer to Berne had majorities in favor of remaining in the old canton. Each community along the new border line could then choose whether it preferred to remain where it ended up, or switch over to the other side. A few switched. Some individuals who were not happy with the new political arrangements moved over to the other side. After that the conflict has largely subsided, and politically motivated violence has stopped. Why not try the same approach in Northern Ireland and other similarly troubled areas? Violence tends to erupt when peaceful change (e.g., through popular referendum) is blocked.

Thich Nhat Hanh:

CAN YOU BE MORE THAN AMERICANS?

In South Africa, the black people suffer enormously, but the white people also suffer. If we take one side, we cannot fulfill our task of reconciliation in order to bring about peace.

Are there people who can be in touch with both the black community and the white community in South Africa? If there are not many of them, the situation is bad. There must be people who can get in touch with both sides, understanding the suffering of each, and telling each side about the other. Are there people doing that kind of understanding and mediation and reconciliation between the two major political blocs on the earth? Can you be more than Americans? Can you be people who understand deeply the suffering of both sides? Can you be the message of reconciliation?

Dorothy T. Samuel:

SOUTH AFRICA: A PROPOSAL FOR PEACEFUL CHANGE

There will, inevitably, be universal enfranchisement in South Africa. Both the terrible delay and the terrible danger spring from the ever-increasing probability of violence and retaliation as the races meet for the first time on a basis of legal equality. The fears of the present white power structure are rooted in recognition that people oppressed for centuries do not gently and gratefully blend into equal relationships long denied them.

Peace people also recognize this historical truth. Therefore, it is most important to move beyond the advocacy of equality while minimizing violence. Such plans require breaking the bonds of traditional political thinking and daring to envision new approaches suitable to contemporary realities and opportunities.

Traditional approaches to enfranchisement have always begun with the men of oppressed groups. And, historically, black men have moved into power with the same violent, macho attitudes and responses that characterized white men who had formerly asserted dominance over them.

In the contemporary world, the education and training of women offers a brave new possibility. Let the enfranchisement of blacks and "coloreds," therefore, begin with the enfranchisement of non-white women. Women are much less likely than men to initiate violence individually or to organize group violence. And from positions of threatened power, frightened white South African males are far less likely to respond instinctively with physical violence against a woman who is opposing them in argument or election, or who is entering a previously restricted café or concert.

Remove all pass laws for women; let women first mingle freely and totally with the white society in businesses, restaurants, theaters, and clubs. Mandate proportional representation for people of color with all the first candidates to be women. Mandate equal-opportunity appointment procedures with all the first black and "colored" appointees to be women. Set up equal opportunity hiring laws with all the first hirees in previously excluded positions to be black and "colored" women. Decree and enforce all the new freedoms for non-white women immediately, and decree and enforce a time limit (ten years perhaps) after which all non-white *people* shall receive the same equality.

Obviously, this will result in many offices of leadership being filled with non-white women before non-white males have opportunities to seek them. This preference position is not the ideal of equality, of course, but it is no more unequal than the historical reverse, and it improves the opportunities for rapid and peaceful integration of all people.

And it utilizes another general characteristic of women. Women could be counted upon to use every bit of power they gain, from the moment they gain it, to hasten the enfranchisement of "their" men, and to improve the conditions of those men in the intervening years. Women are unhappy with any advantages "their" men do not share.

Unfortunately, enfranchised men of any color have never embraced such a primary concern to provide equal advantages for "their" women.

If peace in the world and on the streets is truly as great a priority as racial equality, all people should prefer that integration take place through the sex least likely to initiate or provoke violence.

Greg Guma:

COOPERATIVE SELF-RELIANCE

The debt crisis in most developing countries has created hunger, disease, and a dependency that threatens not only the economic, but also the environmental stability of the entire planet. To meet the terms of international lenders, many poor nations must make cutbacks in the public sector and submit to multinational development strategies stressing resource extraction, one-crop agriculture, deforestation and exports, over the meeting of local needs.

It will not be easy to reduce the estimated $1 trillion debt of the developing nations, but the non-aligned movement has pioneered an approach that will certainly help: action-oriented solidarity and mutual cooperation. In southern Africa, the war between the frontline states and South Africa has led to two promising efforts. The South African Development Coordination Conference (SADCC) is an association of states working together on development projects that will reduce dependency on South Africa.

AFRICA (Action Fun for Resistance to Invasion, Colonialism, and Apartheid) was established by the non-aligned movement in 1987 to provide a wide variety of economic aid, with pledges from members of the movement. Both assist African countries to obtain goods, services and transportation from one another.

The overall strategy is to depend less on industrial nations and turn instead toward collective self-reliance and regional cooperation. Efforts already underway include regional trade through a preferential market involving customs reductions on specific items, liberalized regional import policies, and mutual aid agreements in areas such as agriculture, telecommunications, industrial countries and multinationals. As Zimbabwe's Robert Mugabe puts it, South-South cooperation and collective self-reliance are "an indispensable and integral part of our efforts to restructure the current unjust and inequitable world economic system."

Gene Knudsen Hoffman:

A STEADY GLOW FROM THE DARK CONTINENT

The Centre for Intergroup Studies has been in Capetown, South Africa, for twenty years. It has fostered the willingness of diverse, opposed groups to talk with one another through its carefully developed skills of mediation and conflict resolution. One of the people responsible for its astonishing successes is its South African Director Hendrik William van der Merwe. He is a soft-spoken Professor of Sociology and a Quaker. ("My wife, son, and I are the only Afrikaans-speaking Quakers in the world.")

"Without him there might not yet be any talks between antagonistic parties: white and black nationalists in South Africa. Today the African National Congress (ANC), now in exile, meets with white business people, students, church leaders, trade unionists, and even the leader of the Broederband, the secret society of the Boers. Probably no other South African may claim to be on such friendly terms with the imprisoned Nationalist leader, Nelson Mandela, as well as Andries Treurnicht, chairman of the right-wing party. Only a few years ago he was called a Communist by the Afrikaners. Today the white government seeks his advice." (*Frankfurter Allgemeine Zeitung*, January 8, 1987)

What has brought about these astonishing relationships? Certainly there is something in the quality of the man himself. He prefers to be an observer and likes to listen, not to preach. He has a strong optimism founded in his deep faith that there is something of God in every person and he can appeal to it. He has renounced violence.

In his own words, "When a system is an intransigent and the laws are as rigid as in our society, the public may resort to civil disobedience. But civil disobedience is by its very definition a negative act. My plea is for a more positive response which I would call 'conscientious affirmation.' This does not necessarily require breaking of any specific law; it requires affirmative demonstration of fellowship, love, tolerance, and a commitment to peace and justice."

(Van der Merwe is flexible and open. He finds some of "South Africa's archaic laws" so objectionable that he cannot obey them with a clear conscience.)

"But apartheid is more than a moral issue of human rights. It is a case of socio-economic exploitation with a *system* or *structure* of inequality. It is also . . . an international issue, since apartheid in South Africa represents a microcosm of the world situation. European and American countries are therefore involved. . . .

"In my travels abroad," he writes, "I have been struck by the powerful unifying *forces of opposition to the evils of racial discrimination*. Those of us concerned with the long-term future of my country must do more than just attack the present evils. We need to build the foundations for a stable future society. In this venture I hope it will be the *unifying forces of support for a just society* that will bind us together.

". . . It is not necessarily valid to surmise that (Apartheid) is being practiced by bigoted, hostile, and intolerant individuals. 'It is not that this is directly willed, rather, it happens that we are collectively part of a system that is operating unjustly,' wrote Father Patrick T. O'Mahony. Moral indignation often encourages victimology... Witch hunts do not contribute towards a better society.

Rather than 'periodic fits of (excessive) morality,' we need a deep commitment to certain methods or means in order to obtain a certain objective. Strategic commitment is an essential element for success... but there are major differences in emphasis between strategic and moral commitment.

"Specific commitment to strategy (often) leads toward intolerance towards people who share one's goals but apply other strategies. It is therefore divisive (and) implies a certain measure of arrogance... Strategic commitment may more likely be motivated by moral indignation than by moral commitment, and moral indignation helps to shape a negative short-term goal—that of destroying the object of our indignation.

"The challenge to us is not to become obsessed with short-term negative goals, but to be steadfast in pursuing ultimate goals of justice and conciliation which cannot be achieved in a white-dominated South Africa. The danger is that the tremendous injustice in my country may arouse in us such moral indignation and negative reaction that we may not only destroy the object of our indignation, but may also destroy our future."

Frances Kendall and Leon Louw:

SOUTH AFRICA:
THE DECENTRALIST ALTERNATIVE

There is only one way in which the wide diversity of social, cultural, ethnic, and political aspirations of South Africans can be accommodated. The country must be divided into states or cantons. To understand why this solution is necessary, it is essential to grasp that the problem is not simply one of a small white minority dominating a large black majority. South Africa's defining characteristic is that of diversity.

South Africa is a unique country with unique problems. Clearly it will have to develop its own solutions. However, we do not have to reinvent the wheel. Switzerland provides us with a remarkably apt working model in which many of the problems facing South Africa today have been confronted and solved over several centuries.

Swiss history has led not to a centralized state, but to small communities of varying size, economic strength, and cultural tradition living voluntarily and in mutual respect in the same federal state. Any future political dispensation of South Africa must clearly be based on a system which ensures that all her disparate groups can live without fear of domination by any other group.

The details of the government are based on the Swiss Model and are carefully spelled out. Here it seems important to deal with areas where South Africa would be different. There are some important advantages to a canton system for South Africa.

The first is that diversity is truly democratic. The greater the diversity the more real choices people have, and the greater the likelihood that they will be able to live in a way that coincides with their own values.

Secondly, people can see from day to day which tax policy, which housing policy, which race policy, which subsidy policy produces the best results.

Thirdly, the question of power-sharing would become a non-issue since central government in a canton system would be so limited that there would be almost no power to share.

The Bill of Rights would be an entrenched provision listing certain fundamental and inviolable rights of all citizens and cantons. It includes the following provisions:

- EQUALITY: No law, practice, or policy of government at any level shall discriminate on the grounds of race, ethnicity, color, creed, gender, or religion.
- CIVIL LIBERTIES: There shall be freedom of speech and freedom of the press, subject only to considerations of public decency and safety according to the norms of the canton or community concerned.
- FREEDOM OF MOVEMENT: All citizens of South Africa may move freely from, into, or through all parts of the country on public thoroughfares and in public places. (This would enable people to leave cantons whose policies did not concur with their own values and move to more congenial ones.)

South Africans are ready for change. The current government has an electoral mandate to bring about real reform, and that is what it must do:

A. A new constitution should be drawn up establishing a cantonal system.
B. Leaders of *all* groups should be consulted while a constitution is drawn up. This means the government must release African National Congress leader Nelson Mandela from jail and un-ban the ANC.
C. South Africans of all races should be given equal rights of citizenship.

D. The new constitution should be put to a popular referendum of all citizens.

Mark Satin:

SARVODAYA: A MOVEMENT THAT WORKS

The most successful decentralist/globally responsible movement in the world today is not in North America, or even Western Europe. It's in the Third World—specifically, in Sri Lanka, off the southern coast of India.

Since 1958, the Sarvodaya movement has gone from a small group of young people, working alongside the very poor, to a people's self-help movement that is active in over 4,000 Sri Lankan villages—operating programs for health, education, agriculture, and local industry, all without government funds. (The word "sarvodaya" means the awakening of all—all people, but also all the levels of a person's being.)

Finally we have an easily accessible source for information about Sarvodaya: Joanna Macy's book, *Dharma and Development* (Kumarian Press, 630 Oakwood Avenue, #119, West Hartford, Connecticut, $7.00 pbk). *Dharma and Development* gives us a good general introduction to the Sarvodaya movement. But its special contribution is to pose the question: Why is the movement so successful? As Macy herself points out, "Its grassroots vitality is something no foreign money can buy and no government program can confer." The movement engages 100,000 full-time workers, only 6 percent of whom receive a living wage. What do they know that we don't?

According to Macy, the roots of people's commitment—the roots of Sarvodaya's success—are to be found in religion.

Sarvodaya organizers don't march into towns and villages and tell people what they "should" believe. Their goals for the movement and the ideas they express are firmly rooted in the religious concepts and values of the Buddhist culture. Sarvodaya succeeds because people respond enthusiastically to a perspective that incorporates their deepest values—even when those values are no longer consciously held.

For example, the Sarvodaya movement has adopted local self-reliance as a development goal. Sarvodaya organizers interpret "self-reliance" in terms of the Buddhist principle that salvation lies primarily in one's own hands.

Is the Sarvodaya experience replicable? In her last chapter, Macy—a board member of Sarvodaya International—answers with a very emphatic *yes*! It is not precisely replicable, of course—much of it is culturally specific—but there are many lessons we can learn from it. For example:

• LISTEN TO THE PEOPLE: Sarvodaya instigates "family gatherings" where the local community itself assesses its needs, determines its priorities, and—not least—listens to itself. Sarvodaya organizers are trained to find value in each person's perspective and experience, whatever their background or level of education.

• INTEGRATE SPIRITUAL AND SOCIAL CHANGE: Sarvodaya is successful partly just because it combines spiritual and political themes. (Could this be a universal longing?)

• RESTORE COLLECTIVE SELF-ESTEEM: "Instead of presenting his movement as a novel endeavor, Sarvodaya founder A.T. Ariyaratne did just the opposite. He rooted Sarvodaya in his people's past, offering it as something familiar but momentarily forgotten. He gave them a past to take pride in—and helped them, thereby, feel more adequate to the future."

As an idealized blueprint for movements, not just in Third World societies but in our own, *Dharma and Development* is unique.

Mark Shepard:

LET THE FOREST RISE

Gopeshwar is the home village of Chandi Prasad Bhatt.
Like most men of the mountains, he had been forced
by a shortage of farmland and jobs to come to the plains to find
work. He was also concerned with the plight of his mountain
people. They lacked farmland and jobs and suffered under an
oppressive government forest policy. The government restricted
huge areas from their use, then auctioned off the trees to lumber
companies and industries from the plains.

In 1956 Chandi Prasad and others organized self-help programs among the villagers. All during the next fourteen years,
their efforts were blocked by the government and the lumber
companies.

In 1970 the mountain people faced another consequence of
official forest policy. The monsoon rains that year flooded the
Alakhnanda River. Hundreds of homes were swept away as
well as five major bridges. Almost 200 people died and all
irrigation and power production was halted.

From this, the villagers learned that clear-cutting of the
forests was the main cause. The workers sent a report of their
findings to the government. It brought no response.

In March 1973, two Simon Company agents arrived in
Gopeshwar to supervise the cutting of trees. When Chandi
Prasad heard this, he declared in desperation: "Let them know
they will not fell a single tree without felling one of us first.
When their men raise their axes, we will embrace the trees to
protect them." He locked his hands together in a gesture of
"Chipko" or embrace.

Several weeks later, the villagers learned the trees were marked to be felled, so they marched out of Gopeshwar, beating drums and singing. When they reached the village just below the marked trees, they held a rally. When the Simon Company agents saw them, they were unnerved and retreated without the trees.

Forest Department officials sought to negotiate with the villagers, but they were unwilling to allow the Simon Company its quota. The Simon Company's permit was cancelled and the trees were assigned to villagers instead.

This was a short-held victory. The Simon Company moved from one forest after another in other parts of the district. Despite threats, intimidation, and trickery, the villagers were determined to save these forests as well. In the following years the "Chipko Movement" as they came to be called, rose many times to save their forests. They had to endure the felling of many more trees and more devastating floods.

One of the demonstrations which brought the exploitation of the forests to an end was at Reni. The government had tricked the men into being away while the lumbermen and Forest Department officials moved into the forest. A little girl saw them and ran to tell Gaura Devi, an elderly leader of village women. Within minutes, about thirty women and children were hurrying toward the forest. They reached the lumbermen's camp. The women pleaded with them to return to the village to talk to the village men.

One of the lumbermen pointed a gun at one of the women. Gaura Devi stood in front of him, bared her breast, and told him he would have to shoot her before she would allow the forest to be cut. The lumbermen agreed to leave the forest.

Some months later, the Chief Minister set up a committee to investigate the situation, and the lumber company withdrew to await the decision. Two years later the committee reported that Reni forest was a "sensitive area" and that no trees would be cut there. However, the trials and successes of the Chipko Movement continued. More forests in other areas were threatened.

Since 1975 the Chipko people have not only been protecting

forest slopes, but have been restoring bare ones as well. In 1978 they planted 100,000 trees and developed methods of forest farming, both to conserve forests and to create employment.

The Chipko movement has sprouted branches in other regions. Its goal, as Chanki Prasad put it, "is not only saving the trees, but the right use of the trees." The movement not only protects the sensitive mountain slopes, but insists that mountain people be given an active part in managing their own forests. They see that the issues of ecology and community rights are closely intertwined with resources . To their cry "Let the forest rise; let the forest people rise!" Chandi Prasad responds: "If you halt the erosion of humankind, humankind will halt the erosion of the soil."

Anonymous:

TRUTH AND THE CONTRAS

This is an anonymous letter from a peaceworker in Nicaragua and Honduras. It was written out of a need to speak that person's truth and the fear that it could be manipulated. It seems to me the writer made a profound and "reconciling choice for peace."

I have always been fearful of describing the contras as humans. My fear is that if I describe them as human beings, my readers will conclude that we should give them more instruments of death. As a Christian and a citizen of conscience I can in no way support what the contras do: they kill children, rape women, and kidnap my friends.

But I am also fearful of failing to describe the contras as humans. I fear that in dehumanizing them we will lose our ability to love and forgive them, for when we dehumanize and demonize people, we quickly justify their destruction. If we are to be true peacemakers, we must see and describe the contras truthfully. . . . So, with the goal of putting a human face on the contras, I have decided to write about my recent encounters with them in the isolated mountains of N.Z.

A Call to Conversion: Through the shadows of the dim candles in the tiny chapel, eight hours walk from the nearest dirt road, I watched the contras shift their AKA rifles from one hand to the other. We had spent most of the afternoon talking, members of the counterrevolution and I. Our conversation was intense and frank.

I knew, from eight months experience in Nicaragua, that the

contras could potentially do anything to me. But once I accepted that, I felt freedom to speak and fearlessness to speak truth.

But I also listened. The contras talked about democracy, the unjust obligatory military service law of the Sandinistas, and the Sandinistas' bombings, which injure and kill civilians in the mountains.

Through the darkness I watched their rifles and grenades. I had been asked to preach this night, and feeling both saddened by so much death and bonded by our frank dialogue, I was moved to speak . . . in the contra-filled chapel about nonviolent love.

Suffering was the theme of the evening reading. As I looked into their respectful dark faces, I saw a desert of suffering: bootless feet, ragged clothes, not enough machetes, too much war . . .

Dark faces sat and camouflage uniforms restlessly stood in the aisle. ". . . You suffer because of war, because bombs fall near your houses, because your relatives are recruited or detained or kidnapped. When we suffer such injustices, we are tempted to revenge. We try to change the war with more war. We respond to violence with more violence, to injustice with more injustice.

"But can we change war by making more war? Can we heal the wounds of violence with more violence?"

"No," an unknown voice responded from the darkness.

"And does God want us to respond to violence with hate and revenge?"

"No," another civilian voice rang out. "We can't make the world better with hate or revenge."

The contras became still and quiet and the words seemed to spread through them like a penetrating wave. Yet I never felt like I was speaking against them . . . I felt like I was speaking about nonviolence because I was sure it was the best thing for everyone.

"I certainly know it is difficult to love our enemies," I continued. "Just a few hours ago I was talking to a (contra) commando about Christian love, and I asked him if he could love his enemies, the dogs (Sandinistas).

At first he said, "Of course, after the triumph I will love all of them."

But I said, "No, can you love them now?"

"Of course not," he said, "We are at war; in war you have to kill."

"It is difficult to love our enemies but there is no other way to change the world. Killing and hate only bring more killing and hate. . . ." I looked at the faces and the rifles in front of me. The message of nonviolent love did seem to be churning within them . . . In their unsettled minds I saw great hope. Yet, sitting there, I was struck by the realization that the call was not only for their conversion. It was also for mine.

I looked into the eyes and behind the AKAs and thought of how many times I had privately wished them evil; how many times I had dehumanized them; how many times I had hoped they would all be killed. I needed conversion as much as they did.

The chapel erupted in song and I silently thanked God for the opportunity to heal my evil thoughts toward the contras; for the chance to listen to their stories and to see their faces. These people do terrible things, I thought. They are misled. But they are also my brothers and sisters. Over the last three days I had been converted.

Two days after I finished my twelve-day trip into the mountains, a group of contras attacked a civilian agricultural cooperative where my co-worker was spending the night. Despite the fact that he was sleeping in a house which contained neither armed personnel nor weapons, the contras shot into the dwelling, wounding a thirteen-year-old girl. As my co-worker wrapped his sweater around her bleeding leg, the contras entered the house and kidnapped him . . .

The contras continue to do terrible things. So I pray that God will give me the love to forgive them, the wisdom to convert them, and the courage to correct those in the U.S. who support them.

Global Ways Out

Thich Nhat Hanh:

RECONCILIATION, NOT VICTORY

During the war in Vietnam, we young Buddhists organized ourselves to help victims of the war rebuild villages that had been destroyed by the bombs. Many of us died during service, not only because of the bombs and the bullets, but because of the people who suspected us of being on the other side. We were able to understand the suffering of both sides, the Communists and the anti-Communists. We tried to be open to both, to understand this side and to understand that side, to be one with them.

That is why we did not take a side, even though the whole world took sides. We tried to tell people our perception of the situation: that we wanted to stop the fighting, but the bombs were so loud. Sometimes we had to burn ourselves alive to get the message across, but even then the world could not hear us. They thought we were supporting a kind of political act. They didn't know that it was a purely human action to be heard, to be understood.

We wanted reconciliation; we did not want a victory. The Communists killed us because they suspected that we were working with the Americans, and the anti-Communists killed us because they thought we were with the Communists . . .

The situation of the world is still like this. People completely identify with one side, one ideology. To understand the suffering and the fear of a citizen of the Soviet Union, we have to become one with him or her. To do so is dangerous—we will be suspected by both sides. But if we don't do it, if we align ourselves with one side or the other, we will lose our chance to work for peace. Reconciliation is to understand both sides, to go to one side and describe the suffering being endured by the other side, and then to go to the other side and describe the suffering being endured by the first side. Doing only that will be a great help for peace.

Gene Knudsen Hoffman:

LOUIS PEREZ AGUIRRE— "MY VENGEANCE"

Louis Perez Aguirre, founder of Servicio Pax Y Justicia (Fellowship of Reconciliation) in Uruguay, wrote in 1984: "It is very important to see the issue of amnesty for political prisoners in Uruguay in the context of reconciliation and forgiveness, because that is the only way to treat crimes against humanity, such as torture, kidnappings, and bloodshed . . . What I mean by reconciliation is breaking the circle of evil, which consists of vengeance and returning evil for evil. Reconciliation lies in ending this apparent logic. It's nothing but the capacity to be human and forgive your enemy. It does not mean denying justice and forgetting about everything . . . If we are to reach a tomorrow with possibilities and live together in peace we must overcome the spirit of rancor and vengeance.

Reconciliation is more than just egalitarian justice, giving both parties what they deserve. It is the capacity to demonstrate the ability of human beings to (overcome) evil.

"Here is an example: Thomas Borges, a member of the governing junta, was visiting the prison where he had been incarcerated only a few months earlier and he met a high official of the Somosista-guard, a person responsibile for the torture he had endured. Borges spoke both to the guard and the people present. 'My first vengeance will be this—that your children and your wife will live in peace and freedom. You see these hands? They are not made to kill, but to care for life.' He then embraced the man and said, 'You are free.' "

Gene Knudsen-Hoffman:

SPEAKING TRUTH TO POWER

S peak truth to power" became a resounding call among us Quakers in the fifties. It brought with it a sense of vast possibilities. It is still a significant call and demands courage and presence in its practice—but it's only half the equation.

Recently I've been thinking about and experiencing the other half: "Listen to power to discover the Truth it speaks."

Within the past year I have made two pilgrimages. One was around the world, visiting peace centers and peace people in troubled areas. The other was across our nation, for the Fellowship of Reconciliation, to speak of what I had learned. I carried with me a talisman from Thomas Merton, "We have to have a deep, patient compassion for the fears and the irrational mania of those who hate."

On both journeys I met with people who feared, people who I thought had irrational responses to dangers today, people who expressed what felt like hatred—and they were people of power.

One example must stand for all. This experience took place at a Jewish temple where the majority were political Zionists. I described the peace movement in Israel and the conditions among the Palestinians which had created it. After my address I was met with abuse, excoriation, threats, certainly fear, and naked hatred. (There was also courageous support.)

I had never met with political Zionists before, and all my reading had not prepared me for the fear and grief which had sealed some of their minds against knowledge of realities between the Israelis and the Palestinians. I had not listened long nor deeply enough.

This contact has led to a meaningful correspondence with the rabbi of the temple. I feel we met as human beings across the wide spaces in thought, philosophy, and belief between us. A way is open for us to continue to explore each other's approaches to life.

My experiences have persuaded me that some of us must begin thoughtful acts of listening to people in power *with no thought of trying to speak our truths.* And I believe we must meet them on their home ground.

There are so many we can meet with. We can meet with the pro-nuclear people, with those who live down our street. We must get out of our safe forums and our seminars and sit down face-to-face with our opposition—with those who manufacture Trident submarines, with people from Westinghouse and G.E., with military people—with whomever God sends our way. This is how we will know there are *people* on the other side of these terrible questions, and so will they.

Then we must listen. We must listen and listen and listen. We must listen for the Truth in our opponent, and we must acknowledge it. After we have listened long enough, openly enough, and with the desire to really hear, we may be given the opportunity to speak our truth. We may even have the opportunity to be heard.

For no one and no one side is the sole repository of Truth.

But each of us has a spark of it within. Perhaps, with compassion as our guide, that spark in each of us can become a glow and then perhaps a light, and we will watch one another in awe as we become illuminated. And then, perhaps, this spark, this glow, this light will become the enlightening energy of love that will save all of us.

Ken and Geraldine Grunow:

SIMULTANEOUS CONCESSIONS:
A Mechanism for Resolving Disputes

Many disagreements cannot be resolved because each party to the dispute insists on a critical concession from the other before it will agree to come to the bargaining table.

There are many examples. Here is one: Israel will not recognize the Palestinians' right to an autonomous homeland before the Palestinians recognize Israel's right to exist; and the Palestinians insist on Israel recognizing their right to an autonomous homeland before they will recognize the state of Israel.

Here is a suggestion for a way out of this deadlock: a meeting room with specially designed entry doors. The two doors are connected to one another by a mechanism that permits entry only when both are being opened at the same time. The disputants are to understand, by the symbolism of opening the doors together, that each is recognizing the other's right (or having its own right recognized) simultaneously.

In this way the disputants *both* are the cause of negotiation, neither side "giving in" to the other. Both save face.

Multiple issues contingent upon one another could be resolved by multiple entrances.

Once in the room, the disputants could begin by sitting down *side by side* to view, say, films on suffering to which they are not party (e.g., the Ethiopian or other famine). This would focus their attention together on fellow feeling for humanity (prompting them to consider the suffering their own policies may be causing).

The next item on their agenda could be a reading out, alternately, of their answers to the following questions: (1.) What have I (my side) done to cause the dispute that brings us here? (2.) What can I do to make it better?

The disputants may then proceed, since they are still seated side by side, to develop a common text stating what "our" problem is and how "we" may resolve it (the "our" and "we" being inclusive language describing the disputants).

Kurt Vonnegut, Jr.:

WAR PREPARERS ANONYMOUS

What has been America's most nurturing contribution to the culture of this planet so far? Many would say jazz. I, who love jazz, will say this instead: Alcoholics Anonymous.

I am not an alcoholic. If I were, I would go before the nearest AA meeting and say, "My name is Kurt Vonnegut. I am an alcoholic." God willing, that might be my first step down the long, hard road back to sobriety.

The AA scheme, which requires a confession like that, is the first to have any measurable success in dealing with the tendency of some human beings, perhaps 10 percent of any population, to become addicted to substances that give them brief spasms of pleasure but in the long term transmute their lives and the lives of those around them to ultimate ghastliness.

The AA scheme, which, again, can work only if the addicts regularly admit that this or that chemical is poisonous to them, is now proving its effectiveness with compulsive gamblers, who are not dependent on chemicals from a distillery or a pharmaceutical laboratory. This is no paradox. Gamblers, in effect, manufacture their own dangerous substances. God help them, they produce chemicals that elate them whenever they place a bet on simply anything.

If I were a compulsive gambler, which I am not, I would be well advised to stand up before the nearest meeting of Gamblers Anonymous and declare, "My name is Kurt Vonnegut. I am a gambler."

Whether I was standing before a meeting of Gamblers Anonymous or Alcoholics Anonymous, I would be encouraged to testify as to how the chemicals I had generated within myself, or swallowed, had alienated my friends and relatives, cost me jobs and houses, and deprived me of my last shred of self-respect.

I now wish to call attention to another form of addiction, which has not been previously identified. It is more like gambling than drinking, since the people afflicted are ravenous for situations that will cause their bodies to release exciting chemicals into their bloodstreams. I am persuaded that there are among us people who are tragically hooked on preparations for war.

Tell people with that disease that war is coming and we have to get ready for it, and for a few minutes there they will be as happy as a drunk with his martini breakfast or a compulsive gambler with his paycheck bet on the Super Bowl.

Let us recognize how sick such people are. From now on, when a national leader, or even just a neighbor, starts talking about some new weapons system that is going to cost us a mere $29 billion, we should speak up. We should say something on the order of, "Honest to God, I couldn't be sorrier for you if I'd seen you wash down a fistfull of black beauties with a pint of Southern Comfort."

I mean it. I am not joking. Compulsive preparers for World War III, in this country or any other, are as tragically and repulsively addicted as any stockbroker passed out with his head in a toilet in the Port Authority bus terminal.

For an alcoholic to experience a little joy, he needs maybe three ounces of grain alcohol. Alcoholics, when they are close to hitting bottom, customarily can't hold much alcohol.

If we know a compulsive gambler who is dead broke, we can probably make him happy with a dollar to bet on who can spit farther than someone else.

For us to give a compulsive war-preparer a fleeting moment of happiness, we may have to buy him three Trident submarines and a hundred intercontinental ballistic missiles mounted on choo-choo trains.

If Western Civilization were a person—

If Western Civilization, which blankets the world now, as far as I can tell, were a person—

If Western Civilization, which surely now includes the Soviet Union and China and India and Pakistan and on and on, were a person—

If Western Civilization were a person, we would be directing it to the nearest meeting of War Preparers Anonymous. We would be telling it to stand up before the meeting and say, "My name is Western Civilization. I am a compulsive war-preparer. I have lost everything I ever cared about. I should have come here long ago. I first hit bottom in World War I."

Western Civilization cannot be represented by a single person, of course, but a single explanation for the catastrophic course it has followed during this bloody century is possible. We the people, because of our ignorance of the disease, have again and again entrusted power to people we did not know were sickies.

And let us not mock them now, any more than we would mock someone with syphilis or smallpox or leprosy or yaws or typhoid fever or any of the other diseases to which the flesh is heir. All we have to do is to separate them from the levers of power, I think.

And then what?

Western Civilization's long, hard trip back to sobriety might begin.

Andrea Ayvazian:

A NEW IDENTITY

One reason hostility grows between nations is because we see "the other" as the enemy. Rather than see other peoples, other cultures, other nations as simply different, they are often portrayed in a dehumanized, objectified fashion so they can be hated and feelings of aggression can be aroused and wars can be fought.

Barriers are built to keep citizens inside a country and to keep "foreigners" out. This aids a bellicose government in generating propaganda about another nation and thereby creating false images and arousing fear.

There might be less violence and injustice in the world if individuals saw themselves as part of the human family, as citizens of the world. The idea is to break down ways that walls are built between people and find ways for individuals to feel their unity with others who may live half-way around the world. One way to foster this feeling of unity and diminish the feeling of separation would be to issue everyone *world passports*—to make us all citizens of the world, living in different countries. World passports would open up travel and people could eventually settle where they wanted to live. People could travel freely to be reunited with friends or family in other countries. People would see that the barriers, walls, checkpoints, and border patrols we have created are manifestations of our own fear and can be dismantled as easily as they were created.

World passports would be issued to every individual worldwide. People would sign a basic agreement that stated that they would uphold human rights, practice nonviolence, and not violate any laws of a certain territory. World passports would serve as one small step to freeing us from a limitation we have created which no longer serves the causes of global peace and justice.

David Hoffman:

THE LAST WAR

In the past, the peace which ended one war has inevitably become a time of preparation for the next one. Rather than acting to prevent a future nuclear conflict, therefore, we need to complete the previous war and give birth to the acknowledgment that there had actually been a *last war*.

If by "peace" all that is meant is the absence of war, then it is equivalently understood as those intervals between wars. The pattern might suggest that not only do wars "cause" peace, but that conversely, peace causes war. So long as we oppose the concepts of peace and war, we remain frozen in a moral argument with little substance and few alternatives. It is the persistent *cycle* of peace and war that must be broken; and no amount of moral outrage or condemnation of war will suffice, for war is only *part* of the picture.

Our impulse to stop war has prevented us from seeing that the problem is also peace. This helps to explain our present excessive preoccupation with disarmament. The problem with disarmament is that it literally begs the question. Dismantling your arms is something you do *after* you've solved the conflict. Demanding that the nuclear powers disarm is like pleading to an alcoholic to be sober, without understanding that it was the conditions of his sobriety that contributed to the alcoholic's drinking in the first place. Even if we succeed in freezing the further production and deployment of new weapons, even if we cut back by half, we must still recognize and address the question: How will we know when the threat of war is over?

It has often been said that World War II was made inevitable by the terms and conditions of surrender and the burden of reparations imposed on Germany at the end of World War I.

Likewise, World War I, which had been dubbed "the war to end all wars," has been explained as resulting from the failure of the "peace" which ended the Franco-Prussian war in 1871. Will the survivors of World War III similarly blame that catastrophe on the inadequate conclusion of WW II? Will they point to the fact that forty-two years after the war, Germany remained occupied and divided, that the victors set up opposing military alliances with huge concentrations of tactical nuclear weapons along their borders, and that a formal treaty of peace with Germany was never signed?

Perhaps what will ultimately be required is the convening of a *World Peace Conference* that would address the problems left unresolved by WW II. So many major wars—Korea and Vietnam are two notable examples—have been fought over artificial borders imposed by the military status quo existing at the conclusion of that war. Perhaps the seemingly intractable conflicts of today, like those over Israel and Afghanistan, could more easily be resolved in the context of a larger set of problems. Most important, though, such a World Peace Conference could declare that war was no longer acceptable for our species and by negotiating a formal end to World War II, plant in the world-mind the notion that there has indeed been a last war.

Harrop Freeman:

FOUR HISTORICAL WAYS OUT

T his generation has had the good fortune to observe three fairly successful nonviolent revolutions (those of Gandhi, King, and Aquino), and at the same time to be in a culture with the religious heritage of nonviolence of Jesus against the powerful Roman imperialists. Each of these nonviolent revolutions was different, but they all raise common questions.

WHAT IS THE THEORY OF NONVIOLENT CHANGE OF SOCIAL-GOVERNMENTAL PATTERNS? Every one of the four movements at which we are looking recognized that you could not challenge a police-military-imperial dictator state with violence. Gandhi's writings are important to this recognition. As a lawyer he knew that violence was "outside the law" because it attempts an overthrow; but a nonviolent struggle is more like speech, and in world public opinion "inside the law" and legal. He had the following of a large colonized people, fairly united religiously and used to the value of suffering. What he needed to accomplish was a negotiated withdrawal of the British from India, leaving all their government structure intact, and if possible, to create civil servants capable of taking over and carrying on government. He succeeded in ending colonialism for the largest colony of all time—the "Jewel of the British Imperial Crown"—India. *The theory asserts that by nonviolent suffering you gain friends and supporters, rather than create enemies.* The theory is well demonstrated in each of the four cases here. Christianity ultimately became the religion of the Roman empire; King's position is acknowledged by a national holiday; Marcos was ousted and Aquino formed a new government accepted, in general, by the world.

MUST THERE BE A RELIGIOUS BASE FOR THE MOVEMENT? One needs to be careful not to push conclusions too far by the word "must." But it is certain that all four revolutions have a sound religious core. Jesus' movement, some would say, was entirely religious—it was based on a refinement of Judaism. Martin Luther King was a charismatic preacher and he used as his instrument the Southern Christian Leadership Council. Gandhi's revolution has sound backing in Hinduism; he drew his lessons from Christian history and the writings of Tolstoy and Thoreau. His notable procedures were religious in the Hindu tradition: prayer, fasting, petition, suffering. King and Aquino drew on their church communities and the ability of the poor to suffer. I would thus venture that for all four a religious component was a "must."

ON WHOM DO NONVIOLENT REVOLUTIONS RELY FOR "CADRES"? The above illustrations answer to some degree our third query. You need those who have "suffered" under the old system, who are now willing to suffer even more for a new one—this usually means the poor, the dispossessed, those considered previously to be of an inferior class or race. *And* you need intellectuals and leaders from the goodwill community. They can interpret the needs for justice, and what the dispossessed must be given, as well as the feasibility of change. Further, they give the sufferers a new sense of their value, a new resolve in the struggle—for they have found a new and powerful ally. Cadre training is also needed. I merely point out that the Fellowship of Reconciliation (pacifists) were called in to train both King and Aquino followers (*Fellowship Magazine,* March, 1987). Gandhi and Jesus were superb trainers in their religious-cultural traditions.

MUST THERE BE A GROWING BACKDROP FOR CHANGE INTO WHICH THIS MOVEMENT FITS? Whether or not there "must" be an overall social-religious change going on, into which this struggle links and from which it derives strength, it is true that each of the four nonviolent successes was born at a time of such change. Jesus and Christianity fit into the world-wide religious upheaval. Surely Gandhi's program came with the first stirring of anti-colonialism, and Aquino's power arose when dictatorships were on their way out. It surely helps to move with a tide!

MUST THERE BE A MARTYR? In all four of our cases there was— Jesus on the cross; Gandhi at the hand of a fanatic; King assassinated at the peak of power; Benigno Aquino killed as he returned home to lead the struggle against Marcos. Surely the general adherents of a cause need a leader. And, as one person remarked: "A dead hero is worth several live leaders."

CAN NONVIOLENCE SUCCESSFULLY INITIATE CHANGE AND YET BE UNABLE TO ADMINISTER A MODERN MILITARY-POLICE-INDUSTRIAL STATE AND REMAIN NONVIOLENT? Comes now the most difficult, and perhaps unanswered, question. In India even Gandhi's closest followers did not continue proposals in the Indian government, and Gandhianism gradually became an internal humanitarian-religious movement.

Jesus did not seek to govern, but later his followers became as converted to power, violence, war, and militarism as any other leaders. The Philippine revolution probably best illustrates the problem of a nonviolently created government. The military still holds great power (some would say the revolution could not have occurred without them) and Cory Aquino must engage in war against the "insurgents" as her military require, rather than negotiate a settlement as she apparently would like. Until we sometime experiment and perfect a truly nonviolent pattern of government, we do not know whether nonviolence can govern in today's legal, police, power politics, military-industrial society.

Amos Gvirtz:

A CALL FOR A
BALANCE OF TRUST

*There are "historical moments," as Amos Gvirtz calls them,
when people are ready to listen and consider ideas which have
been germinating through the ages. We, of the nonviolent
movement, must see ourselves as cultivators and carriers of an
idea whose time—he believes—has come.* —ED.

Violent conflict created the idea of security through
strength. This is because throughout history the only
response to conflict was greater and greater strength, more and
more powerful armies and weapons—and more clever tricks to
defeat the enemy. With the advance in technology, weapons
became the key to greater strength. It is not difficult to see the
dark logic that begins with violence as a means of security and
ends with the creation of nuclear weapons.

Yet it is precisely this logical progression that created the
ultimate paradox of our time: the weapons that were created for
"total security" have brought the ultimate and total danger.
Security now means total threat.

The progression toward this paradox is by no means unique.

Any idea can be reduced to absurdity when pursued to its
logical extremes. A totally consistent and believing vegetarian,
for example, will be forced to deny her right to existence
because her life itself presents a threat to other living organisms.
The difference between "vegetarianism" and "security," however, is crucial. The vegetarian's paradox threatens only herself,

while the paradox of "total security" carries with it a threat to all life.

The answer is to change our conception of security, to change to one which does not endanger others. I propose a new orientation for security. I propose we move from a "security by fear" to a "security of trust." In a security of "trust" both sides to a conflict will know that their existence and their essential interests are not endangered. This can be accomplished only through nonviolent methods of security, and conflict-resolution.

But what does it mean to advocate a form of security and defense which is nonviolent? Pacifists must find an answer to the very real problems of criminal behavior, the treatment of mentally ill people, and the use of a police force. As I see it, the basic question for the peace movement has always been: "What do *we* do about injustice and violence?"—not "How can large societies maintain nonviolence?" We do have some models as resources. We need to examine them.

We have both historical and contemporary examples. The Quakers ran a government in Pennsylvania for about seventy years without an army. Abdul Ghaffer Khan created an actual nonviolent army in his struggle against the British in what is now Pakistan and Afghanistan. Vinobe Bhave succeeded in bringing about nonviolent land reform in India. All these examples and many more can provide some answers.

Another approach is *Preventive Nonviolence*. We in the American peace movement are familiar with *Active Nonviolence*; we do not have much experience with *Preventive Nonviolence*. How do we prevent potential conflicts from developing into violent conflicts?

The best example I know of Preventive Nonviolence was the behavior of the British Quakers when they arrived in the new land, later to be called Pennsylvania. The potential conflict of war with the Indians was prevented because the Quakers treated the Indians as equal to themselves.

These questions I raise are presented by one who does not have clear answers. I hope to direct our creative thought to these problems—especially the problems of pacifist *responsibility* for the maintenance of society, and not only pacifist criticism of existing leaders. This weakness of ours was highlighted in the case of Gandhi and Nehru when the problems turned from those of fighting the government to those of *becoming* the government. Until we pacifists are willing and able to take on the questions that a lawmaker or government must face, we haven't really addressed ourselves to the central issues of modern peace-making.

Gene Knudsen-Hoffman:

AN ALTERNATIVE TO TERRORISM?

Recently a group of us met to seek a nonviolent alternative to terrorism. This is the recommendation which emerged:

None of us knows why people commit acts of terrorism. It appears to us they are performed when people's frustration tolerance has reached zero, when they feel they are not heard and their grievances will *never* be addressed. Often when such despair takes over, people resort to violence. This is our speculation—and it appears to contain truth.

Our conclusion: What if we declared amnesty for all terrorists and invited them (or a spokesperson for them) to appear anonymously on radio, TV, and other media to tell us why they performed such acts. Our sense is, if we understood why acts of terrorism are committed, we could learn what we need to do to prevent them. We certainly won't be wiser if we remain ignorant.

We feel that perhaps many more lives would be saved

through using this process than through punishment and further violence.

Mary Cotton:

TERRORISM:
SOME HEALING ALTERNATIVES

George Lopez, co-editor of a recent anthology on terrorism, is convinced that the new terrorism is qualitatively different from the old. "... it is not meant to 'wake the masses,' ... to make political demands or to assert political rights. It is basically just for punishment. For example, to punish the Israelis."

Abdul Asiz Said, Professor of International Relations at the American University in Washington, D.C., has this to say of it: "Terrorism has sharpened our words, but not our understanding; Muslims have been saying they want respect, freedom, legitimacy. But that's not what the West sees. The West sees Islamic revival as a threat to Western civilization. . . . The rules and practices of present day world politics are largely Western in form and content. The West is outraged now because terrorists don't play by the rules. However, the rules favor the West . . ."

What might change this?

Abdul Said continues: "Terrorism is understood by disempowered people to accomplish political objectives not possible in the existing environment of world politics . . . Terrorism highlights the lack of . . . a grievance procedure, social change, and law and order in world politics.

"The remedy to terrorism requires the creation of regional

and international standards to promote greater social justice and provide workable institutional mechanisms for dealing with terrorism."

George Lopez, referred to above, suggests we need the following:

An *International Criminal Court* that could hear cases brought by "non-governmental actors" against former heads of state, corporations, individuals, etc.

A general commitment to bringing non-governmental political actors into *some form of dialogue* with national actors in regional and international organizations.

An *International Grievance Agency* to act as low-level intervenor in disputes and also to provide a redress procedure for forms of State terror.

An *International Mediation Agency* that would "attempt to resolve disputes such that states and citizens might not 'need' to resort to violence as a means of conflict resoluton."

A *United Nations Commission for Human Rights* that would provide the means for citizens and groups to hold national leaders accountable for violations of the Universal Declaration of Human Rights.

Kirkpatrick Sale, author of *Human Scale* and *Dwellers in the Land,* has this to say: "I don't know of any terrorists that are not fighting for some kind of homeland. . . . You can solve the problem by dividing (nations) so that each of the groups that feels it has to have a homeland gets a homeland.

"Instead of trying to maintain an overlarge collection of various peoples, thus groups that are truly nations, you allow each region to de-link itself—have its autonomy—develop its territory as it wants to . . .

"We need to take off the blinders of nationalism that insist that nations are permanent, that they cannot be dismantled. We would eliminate most of the terrorism in the world, plus most of the wars if we agreed to the principle of division . . . Most (wars) . . . are being fought by groups not even wanting to take over the State, but wanting to achieve a measure of autonomy *from* the State, like the Basques, or the Tamils in Sri Lanka."

Joanna Macy, Buddhist, creator of Despair and Empowerment Workshops, author of the classic little book on the third world, *Dharma and Development,* speaks: "Terrorism is the avenue for feeling our interconnectedness with all beings; it's a vehicle for teaching Americans what it's like to be afraid . . . This is a time when societies are dislocating; the old is passing. Fear stalks the streets, the refugee camps, the airports. And the people are trying to slip through borders. And the people being hunted. And those who are waiting for their sons and daughters to come home—waiting to see if they'll join 'the disappeared.'

"And fear stalks the farms. Farm families are asking, 'Can we make payments on the debt?' . . . There's a fear of losing everything.

"The terrorists make us afraid and all I know to do about it, on an emotional level, is to see that this is an invitation to experience a little of the gut-wrenching fear that shadows the lives of our brothers and sisters at this moment in time.

"I think there's going to be fear walking all the alleyways and corridors of power until we find ways of sharing the resources of our planet more justly . . .

"I got a beautiful letter just now from a guy who's doing mediation work between the Tamil terror groups and the Sri Lanka government. He says he sees no other way but for each side to see the other as human beings and not as demons."

David Spangler, a spiritual leader and teacher, author of the book *Emergence: The Rebirth of the Sacred,* wrote: "It is important to speak to the dangers inherent in the feeling of homelessness and rootlessness. People are in pain all over the world. That generates a kind of psychic pain that's crying out: There's a lot of pain within the collective unconscious. The existence of refugees who are, in effect, homeless, and have no structure or sense of belonging to a place, creates an entry point through which this psychic pain can enter the world.

"Precisely because these people don't have homes of their own they have no investment in the concept of home. They may wish to reclaim their homeland. But in the present situation, not having a homeland, they don't have a sense of a need to honor the homeland of others.

". . . I feel that what the [terrorist phenomenon] is calling for is a return to a deeper valuing of home and place; and on the other hand, a deeper valuing of the earth as our home. And global institutions that can act out of that perspective."

And finally—this article was written for those who believe that the spectrum of opinion is more like a circle than a straight line. It was written for those who believe that each of the different perspectives on terrorism has something to add to the whole.

Coming up with a solution to terrorism is not a matter of adopting the "correct" political beliefs. It is, rather, a matter of learning to listen—really *listen*—to everyone in the circle of humankind. And to take their insights into account. For everyone has a true and unique perspective of the whole.

Clifton Anderson:

PEACE HAPPENS IN MOSCOW, IDAHO
Seeing the Human Dimension of World Problems

Our foreign visitor enjoyed seeing the rolling hills of Latah County. We spent the morning discussing crops, machinery, and markets with farmers and learning about 4-H clubs from three remarkable, talented girls who live in a century-old farmhouse near Genesee, Idaho.

Lunch was waiting for us at the home of Howard and Mary Jones. Mary had prepared many good things. She had told her four little daughters about our visitor—Vladimir Zvyagin, a Soviet radio-television reporter in New York City. They gave him an enthusiastic welcome.

The friendship displayed by those sparkling, bubbling pre-teen girls was the genuine article. We eleven residents of Moscow, Idaho, who were Vladimir's hosts for the day, realized we were being outmatched by the youngsters. During the next four days, as I introduced Vladimir Zvyagin to dozens of people in the area, I noted many expressions of American-Soviet friendship but none had the same enthusiastic, straight-from-the-heart quality as the welcome these children extended to our Soviet visitor.

As a hard-headed journalist, trained to seek out facts and to shy away from sticky emotions, I'm usually not inclined to gush about childhood's innocence. And I've always been distrustful of revivalists who use the "you-must-become-as-a-little-child" argument. Still, in facing facts, I am ready to grant that psychological realities can be as meaningful as physical realities.

I'm convinced that a psychology of peace is emerging in many regions of the world. It could spread throughout the U.S. and the USSR, smoothing away our mutual fears and animosities, if only we Americans and Soviets would resolve to escape from the numbing psychology of distrust that has paralyzed us for so long. If we would develop bonds of trust, friendship, and empathy, our political differences would still exist, but they would no longer have so great a potential for engulfing our world in a nuclear holocaust.

Beautiful, bright-eyed children have no difficulty accepting the psychology of peace. It is, after all, their natural habitat. Only in a symbolic sense will children be the world's peacemakers, however. We adults have the responsibility for resolving the U.S.-USSR impasse and other global problems. These problems are not just disputes about power, territory, and ideology; at the center, the difficulties revolve around human beings and their views of each other. One thing we should learn from our young children is how to share with others the joyous, exhilarating experiencing of our common humanity!

Vladimir Zvyagin came to Moscow, Idaho, at the invitation of the William E. Borah Foundation for the Outlawry of War. Each year, the foundation sponsors the Borah Symposium at the University of Idaho. For a three-day program examining Soviet-American relations, we arranged for a panel of speakers that included diplomats, journalists, political scientists, historians, and leaders of citizen groups promoting intercultural friendship and cooperation.

As chairman of the Borah Foundation, I worked with a committee of professors and students in planning the symposium. In our early discussions of the U.S.-USSR topic, we spoke a lot about the threats to peace emanating from Moscow, USSR. Later, in a more reflective mood, we began to wonder if all things were as they should be in Moscow, Idaho.

It was at this point that we resolved to develop the symposium along the following lines:

1. As in previous years, we would have an important international issue explored by well-known experts. However, we would endeavor in every way possible to relate the U.S.-USSR issue to the immediate concerns of the people in our community.

2. Using modern technology, could we arrange for a direct communication link between Moscow, Idaho, and Moscow, USSR? Teleconference, transmitted by satellites, would break our budget, but conference via slow-scan television would, we discovered, be within our reach. Two-way sound and images for slow-scan are carried over telephone circuits at overseas rates that are quite reasonable. Joel Schatz, a pioneer in instituting people-to-people linkages between the U.S. and the Soviet Union, arranged three highly successful Moscow-to-Moscow teleconferences.

3. We decided to conclude the symposium with a discussion of this question: What can ordinary citizens do to promote peace? Citizen-diplomats who have contributed to Soviet-

American understanding were invited to participate. Joel Schatz was one participant. Others were Nancy Graham of the Institute for Soviet-American Relations, Cynthia Lazaroff of the U.S.-USSR Youth Exchange Program, Rosanne Royer of the Seattle-Tashkent Sister City Program, and Douglas Mattern of the World Citizens Assembly. These speakers agreed that U.S. citizens today have a wide range of opportunities to work with Soviet citizens in projects promoting peace and understanding.

4. At all stages of our symposium we endeavored to reach out beyond the campus community. We arranged small face-to-face meetings so local people could get acquainted with the citizen-diplomats and also with Vladimir Zvyagin and other symposium speakers.

Our symposium was a success. For many local residents, it was a watershed event, a real "happening." Afterward, they no longer felt so isolated from the arena of citizen diplomacy. Instead, they had a feeling of empowerment—an assured realization that they could reach out in peace to Soviet citizens. Having met some interesting, non-threatening U.S. peace activists, they were encouraged to work actively on behalf of U.S.-USSR friendship.

It remains to be seen if Moscow, Idaho, and Moscow, USSR, have indeed moved any closer together than they were before. Four months after the symposium, these interesting developments had occurred:

—Jay Shelledy, publisher of the local newspaper, *Idahonian*, arranged a Moscow-to-Moscow exchange of journalists. A reporter from his staff went to the Soviet Union for several weeks, and a Soviet editor came to Idaho.   Several other U.S. newspapers are now participating in similar exchanges.

—A group of University of Idaho students proposed to set up student exchanges with the Soviet Union. The group also wants to sponsor slow-scan Moscow-to-Moscow teleconferences several times each year.

—Another group of students intends to invite Soviet musicians to take part in the annual Moscow Jazz Festival.

—Farmers who grow peas and lentils are trying to establish bonds of cooperation with the Soviet pea and lentil industry. They want to set up an information exchange, a program for cooperation in scientific research, and an exchange of germ-plasm for genetic research.

—Mayor Gary Scott and other community leaders will be touring the Soviet Union soon. They will be travelling as private citizens, not as public officials, and all interested citizens may join the tour. This is the first time a proposed tour of the Soviet Union has drawn community-wide participation.

I'm certain that positive actions have a multiplication effect. Each time citizens work together on a project to improve international understanding and cooperation, their example inspires other groups of citizens to begin additional projects. In this way, the psychology of peace will become established in the U.S., in the Soviet Union, and in all other countries.

In the U.S., the number of citizens working to promote U.S.-Soviet friendship is approaching a "critical mass." For individuals who wish to organize friendship projects in their communities, many suggestions are available from the organizations that are concerned with arms control, intercultural education, citizen exchanges, and peace and justice issues.

Outside the formal organizational structures, individuals committed to peace are linked together in an informal communications network. To plug into this network, simply write a letter or make a telephone call to a peace activist and request information about a specific project or activity. Nine times out of ten the person you approach will either give you the facts you need or refer you to someone who has the information. In this struggle for peace, you are not alone!

Richard Wendell Fogg:

PROTECTION FROM NUCLEAR THREATS

W e will probably never stop relying on nuclear weapons until we have an alternative system of defense. A promising system exists—the synthesis of all forms of force with the omission of the nuclear or even the military form. These include political, economic, psychological, and moral forms. We need to determine whether we can extend that defense to protect us in general from threats backed by nuclear weapons.

The challenge of defending ourselves against nuclear threats without using nuclear weapons has not been carefully studied. These proposals seek to bridge the gap.

PRACTICAL EXPERIENCE

A Nation Liberated by Noncooperation. Non-military force was actually strong enough to help bring an area out of Soviet orbit; few people expect military force to achieve this. The Soviets could find or force no Austrian to form an indigenous puppet government as they did in their Eastern European satellites. Ambassador Sven Allard has written that Austrians exposed and shamed countrymen who had received a Soviet offer to form a puppet government so they refused it. Partly because of this refusal to cooperate, the Soviets allowed Austria to become neutral.

Nazis stopped by Active Intervention: Non-military force has not only kept amenable people from achieving *theirs.* Scandinavia used this defense to keep thousands of Jews from being sent to concentration camps; 6,800 of 7,300 Jews in Denmark were saved. One technique of non-military force was alternative government. Gene Keyes, a specialist in civilian-based defense, tells us that the Danes had two national councils; one a "sacrificial goat" to the Nazis, provided apparent capitulation. The auxiliary council ran much of the resistance.

Army stalemated by Threat-Avoidance and Unity: Although no one would expect the Czechoslovakian Army to defeat the Soviet Army in battle, with non-military defense the Czechs did force that army to withdraw its tanks from the battlefield and, after three days, to rotate thousands of its soldiers back to their homeland. In 1968 the Soviets invaded Czechoslovakia. They were surprised to find that the Czech Army stayed in the barracks. Instead civilians dealt with the Soviet troops. According to Professor Gene Sharp, a leading authority on civilian-based defense, the Czechs showed them that they had been misled into believing that there was an uprising and made their tanks a symbol to create Czech unity against them. As a result, many of the Soviet troops malingered and had to be rotated back to their country, and the tanks were returned or hidden.

The Soviets took eight months to topple the Dubcek government—an amazing sixty times longer than the four days they had estimated it would take to do so if they had met the Czech army. The defense ultimately failed, but, of course, we can learn from failures. The Czech non-military defense was spontaneous; had it included years of training, organizing, and funding, it probably would have been even stronger.

At the center for the study of conflict, we study historical cases such as the above to find ways in which non-military defense might apply to nuclear threats. These cases suggest how we could synthesize billions of dollars worth of all the forms of force-without-arms, including political, economic, strategic, psychological, legal, and moral force. So far we have developed a repertoire of about two dozen strategies and tactics applicable by nuclear powers and by countries wanting to avoid becoming nuclear powers.

Persuasions by Avoidance of Nuclear Retaliation, by Discus-

sion of all Grievances, and Invocation of a Taboo: Deterrence theory depends on a policy of the "rationality of irrationality," a concept explained by Herman Kahn . . . This means, as in the game of "chicken," that our president is supposed to give the impression to adversaries that he is irrational enough to use nuclear weapons when fall-out and counterstrike could kill millions of innocent Americans and others. Thus, to the extent that our policy of nuclear deterrence is a bluff, it lacks power; to the extent that it is not, it risks escalation.

By contrast, in a crisis, a declaration that we could *not* retaliate with nuclear weapons even if attacked with them, could, paradoxically, have a strong power to deter. That could be true when (the) government which made a nuclear threat justified it by their belief that we pose a nuclear danger to them. If we were to give strong evidence that we do not; if we were to agree to discuss whatever grievances a leader would claim in order to gain support for his or her threat; and if that threat were to be revealed, then we could undercut it from within and break the adversary's unity . . . Just as it is possible to divide and conquer, so it is possible to divide and defend.

Our pledge not to counter-threaten might have the power to evoke . . . (worldwide) condemnation. If the threat were such that the world would regard it as violating a taboo against nuclear threats and would insist that the adversary withdraw it, that insistence . . . could be more powerful than a nuclear counterthreat by us.

General strike: We could hold a brief, symbolic, government sponsored general strike . . . and we could organize a brief boycott of the adversary wherever possible. We could announce that these actions mean that we have the unity and discipline to struggle with non-military defense.

The Poles used a general strike with great effect in the spring of 1981. At that time, Solidarity announced plans for such a strike of unlimited duration for major goals and then, to prove its determination, held one for fifteen minutes for very minor goals. One was to secure a government apology for the police having been brutal to three Solidarity members. . . . The problem was routine and not worth the millions the brief general strike might cost. But Solidarity used the event to demonstrate its unity and discipline by calling a strike for such a minor matter. This demonstration forced the government to capitulate on the goals of (a) proposed subsequent strike, which was then called. The ultimate purpose of the strike was to help keep the Soviet Army out of Poland, showing the Soviets, in the words of one Solidarity member, that they would have to send enough soldiers to control every Pole on a one-to-one basis. The strike may have been part of what achieved this purpose.

The symbolic, short general strike is a very, very powerful tool available (even) to government leaders. It can mean anything they say it means, including the determination to resist a nuclear threat. The symbolism could also mean the willingness to make the country inoperative and difficult to exploit economically. Such a strike could deter occupation.

SIGNIFICANCE OF THE PROPOSAL

We must discover whether, ultimately, we can make nuclear weapons obsolete by forging all the kinds of force without arms into a more powerful defense that allows a people to be let alone by aggressors (and) that turns morality into power by invoking a taboo against nuclear weapons . . . Indeed, if non-military defense is effectively used, we probably *can* reduce the chance of nuclear war, for the forces of peace have allies among all peoples and all sizeable leadership groups.

Defense . . . without weapons doesn't require complete unity; it requires techniques, practice, high morale, and realization of the danger the bomb poses. The lack of sufficient research on this powerful non-nuclear defense keeps us dependent on a large nuclear arsenal, which probably risks disaster more than would protection by a well-developed non-military defense.

David Hoffman:

GREEN ZONES

Warfare no longer serves as an instrument for the resolution of conflicts between states, and therefore in the twentieth century war itself must be abolished, as slavery was abolished in the nineteenth century.

To accomplish this we will have to shift the context of the disarmament debate from the issue of techno-military superiority to the concept of security, which is a deeper and more fundamental concern. With all of our astronomical spending on atomic hardware, we have nothing with which to defend ourselves against a Soviet attack. (Nor do the Soviets against us!)

A new paradox has developed: the less weapons an area has, the more secure it is; the more weapons surrounding you, the more likely you are to be an undefended target. In fact, the only defense is not to have a defense. As Robert Fuller has pointed out "... to be feared is to be in jeopardy. By instilling fear in others, you diminish your own safety. If you would feel safe, attend to the safety of others. The ancient ethical prescriptions common to all religions become self-enforcing in a nuclear world."

This is my argument for the creation of nuclear-free zones, (many areas, including the Scandinavian countries, are proposing they be declared nuclear-free zones), and a call for a "nuclear-free Europe," sponsored by the European Nuclear Disarmament (END) organization, is generating surprising support.)

The "Green Zone Theory" would extend this logic to the

internal territory of the superpowers themselves. An agreement by both sides would delineate certain areas of equivalent size and importance to be free of any offensive weapons, production facilities, or research laboratories. These areas would then be declared nuclear-free zones, and each power would formally agree not to target them. Each side would retain the same number of nuclear weapons as before. The only change would be a shift in consciousness. Alongside the familiar maps that show likely targets in each country, there could be one marked in green that would be officially untargeted.

Instead of negotiating a limitation in weapons systems, megatonnage or the like, we could negotiate geographically. Once the smallest Green Zone was established, it would be possible to negotiate enlargements or additional Green Zones. Eventually whole regions could demilitarize, nuclear weapons sites could be moved or be dismantled, and progress could be graphically understood by a glance at a map.

What has been complex, technical and secret could be replaced by something simple and obvious. Domestic support for such a proposition would be relatively easy since there would be no reduction in the "defensive" capabilities of either side.

Once the smallest area was designated as a non-target zone, all the unincluded regions would become more conscious of their vulnerability. (It is this awareness that is absolutely essential in the creation of a context where qualitative arms reduction is possible.)

For arms control to work, it must be rooted in the mass consciousness. The establishment of mutually guaranteed Green Zones could make the citizens of the superpowers more acutely aware of how they are undefended fodder in the strategic calculations of deterrence, while simultaneously demonstrating the possibility of agreement for mutually assured security.

One of the more subtle advantages of the Green Zone strategy is that it helps localize a problem which otherwise is elusively abstract and unimaginable. The Green Zone process not only is easily understandable to the lay person, it is also completely nonpartisan. It is one way for the superpowers to reach an agreement that ostensibly reduces the sphere of destruction without reducing "security."

Because it is nonpartisan and therefore avoids the resistance of security-conscious conservatives, the Green Zone theory may rapidly develop a consensus where more traditional arms limitation agreements may not. Such a consensus could go a long way in changing the context from "which side is stronger" to a search for mutually assured security. If it can avoid the fear that is endemic to any proposal for disarmament and yet take a constructive step, no matter how small, toward resolving our suicidal enmity, the world will be better off. Once established and recognized, the green outline on the map could shift the climate of opinion to the pursuit of survival.

Mary Cotton:

TINY LOANS TO
THE WORLD'S POOR

A new approach to helping the world's poor is taking place in obscure corners of the Third World. Rather than giving money to Third World governments and their massive national developmental projects, and then hoping that some of it reaches the poor, the idea is to give or lend money to private, voluntary organizations (PPO's) in the third world, which would then *lend* money—in tiny ($50-$60) chunks—to the poorest of the poor.

The idea is to induce development "from the bottom up," not just from the top down.

This new approach is being developed by Dr. Muhammed Yunus, an economics professor from Chittagong University.

Dr. Yunus started the Grameen Bank in Bangladesh in 1976. It began, according to Mary Connell, as a "pilot project among the landless poor of a village near the university campus. It has since broadened to include over 250,000 borrowers, all of them people owning less than a half-acre of land and 60 percent of them women. The repayment rate has been above 95 percent. Money comes from the U.N. Development Program, the International Fund for Agricultural Development, the governments of Norway and Sweden, and (private foundations).

"Yunus describes the Grameen project as an attempt to reverse the age-old vicious circle of 'low income, low savings, low investment, low savings' into an expanding system of 'low income, credit, investment, more income, more credit, more investment, more income.'

"The basic unit of the scheme is a group of five unrelated people, all of the same sex and from similar circumstance. They come together initially with a bank worker for training and to elect leaders.

"Among themselves, the group members talk out ideas for generating income. They then pick which ideas, and which borrowers, hold the most promise. Initially, two of the five are given small loans (the average loan is $60, which is close to half of the per capita income), with a short payback period. After six weeks, if payments are on schedule, the next two borrowers are eligible, and six weeks later the last borrower.

"Each group member thus has an interest in the success of all the others—which not only adds peer pressure for prompt repayment, but also leads group members to keep a critical eye on the ideas and prospects of others.

"The loans finance a long list of small income-generating projects, including cows, small shops, sewing machines, weaving, fishnet production, food processing, and trading ventures of all kinds.

"Along with borrowing is a forced savings scheme, with each member contributing one *takka* (about a third of a day's wage) to the group savings each week. This money can be borrowed, interest-free, by group members for personal emergencies. Additionally, a 5 percent tax is taken out of each development loan, which then becomes the group's operating fund.

"[The five-person] groups come together into a 'center,' or collection of ten groups, for weekly meetings. The centers scrutinize loan requests, work directly with the bank staff, and also conduct other activities such as building schools. Loan decisions, disbursements, and repayments all take place, not at a bank facility, but at the weekly center meetings.

"[Their] decisions represent a collective effort to improve living conditions. They fulfill another purpose of the development effort identified by Yunus: to bring people within the folds of some organizational format which they can understand and operate and can find socio-political and economic strength in it through mutual support."

Dietrich Fischer:

ACCESS TO OIL

I t has been argued that modern industrial states cannot defend themselves only at their borders. They depend vitally on foreign raw materials, and must defend these "lifelines" just as vigorously as their territory, it is said. This sort of thinking has led to the rapid deployment force and the Carter Doctrine, reaffirmed by Reagan, that the United States was prepared to use any amount of force (presumably including first use of nuclear weapons) to defend its access to Middle Eastern oil. But access to oil cannot be defended with military force. It is impossible to patrol an oil pipeline for hundreds of miles, twenty-four hours a day, seven days a week. A determined group of saboteurs can blow it up, and can do so repeatedly. And the use of nuclear weapons, which might well escalate into a global nuclear war, could, in Richard Barnet's words, "vaporize that oil along with the civilization that depended on it." The United States could make itself less vulnerable against an oil embargo by doing more intensive research on alternative sources of energy, and energy conserving technologies. It could also save some of its Alaskan oil for an emergency and import foreign oil as long as it is available. Most of all, what keeps oil flowing is not the threat or use of force, but incentives for the people who control the oil to sell it. If we have something attractive to offer in return, this is a much better guarantee that oil will keep flowing than if we threaten war. Consumers have long recognized that. Using the "lifeline" argument, we might as well say that if bread is vital to our survival, we should go to the baker not with money to pay but with a gun to make sure we get what we need. If we pursued that approach in our daily lives, we all know that we might cut them short. Why do our leaders think that such a short-sighted suicidal policy makes sense for a nation?

Daniel Deudney:

STAR TREK: A POSITIVE ALTERNATIVE

E ven though the intellectual case against Star Wars is compelling, political and cultural momentum seems to be on the side of its supporters. Why? One reason stands out: the nature of the peace movement in the U.S. today. The peace movement will never be able to counter Star Wars with the same old arguments it has used against nuclear power and nuclear weapons.

To compete with the seductive appeal of Star Wars, the peace movement will have to lay aside its anti-technological ethos. It must steer, rather than brake, technology. The peace movement cannot simply stop technological momentum head-on, but must instead try to channel that momentum away from programs like Star Wars. *Unless it develops a positive agenda for the cooperative use of space technology, the peace movement will be no more successful in halting the arms race in space than it has been in halting the arms race on earth.*

We don't need Star Wars, but we do need a joint U.S.-Soviet "Star Trek"—and it is not just a pipe dream.

A large-scale program for space cooperation—Star Trek instead of Star Wars—is a complement, not an alternative, to arms control and disarmament. But it could make a powerfully important "Breakthrough"-type contribution to global security.

—Star Trek could provide an outlet for the energies and technologies now lavished on doomsday devices—for it would surely capture the imagination of those now attracted to the high tech/high adventure aspects of Star Wars.

—Star Trek could link the most technologically advanced sectors of both societies in common—and useful—tasks.

—Large-scale U.S.-Soviet cooperation could create its own momentum.

—Four decades of arms buildup cannot simply be reversed. The process of constructing a global security system and establishing less antagonistic relations between the superpowers must begin *while,* not *after,* the goals of arms control and arms reductions are pursued.

—The peace movement currently gathers much of its grassroots support from those who want to divert resources away from the military and into social reconstruction. But most military conversion schemes fail to provide a credible role for the aerospace industry. You can easily envision tank factories turning out tractors. But ICBM manufacturers turning out subways? Fortunately, many of the technologies planned for use in space warfare could readily find a place in peaceful, cooperative space activities . . .

Community activists have tended to view the space program as expendable—as competitor for scarce resources that could be better spent helping the poor and rebuilding the public infra-structure. The peace movement has failed to come up with a cooptive strategy toward space technology—in part because of its technophobic cultural values. But just as leading thinkers in the environmental movement abandoned pastoralist visions of a post-industrial society and embraced certain types of high technology, so too the peace movement must develop a vision of a post-nuclear world that includes a positive role for advanced technology. Otherwise the peace movement will increasingly be relegated to a position of impotent negativism.

Space activists' views have increasingly become unhinged from reality, vacillating between escapist fantasies and visions of sweeping panaceas. What is ironic and sad about its prepos-terous scenarios is that by wildly exaggerating space technol-ogy's near-term potential, they have obscured the ways in which space technology could be used to help solve political conflicts and preserve the habitability of "spaceship Earth."

Today's nuclear abolitionists will have trouble advancing their vision until an alternative system for ensuring security and resolving disputes has been pioneered. Because Star Trek offers a *practical* way to promote U.S.-Soviet cooperation and create the beginnings of an alternative security system, it deserves a central place in peace movement strategy.

Greg Guma:

USE OF OUTER SPACE

Satellite technology is deeply affecting the lives of all people, especially in less-developed countries. Satellites are bringing education and development, as well as increased government control, to previously isolated regions. They provide long-distance phone service in backward areas and new global links for business services. Moreover they can compensate for environmental limitations that disrupt "conventional" communication.

But use of the Geostationary Orbit (GSO) also opens up the possibility of information control by national elites, working with corporate partners, leading to monopoly power over whole regions. The World Bank, aerospace corporations, and the U.S. are already assuming an active role in shaping the Global Telecommunity.

In the next decade, the uses of outer space will challenge traditional concepts of nationalism, sovereignty, and security. Technologies will be available for both peaceful and aggressive purposes, for human freedom, or more sophisticated manipulation. A satellite can monitor the deployment of weapons, or it can be rigged as a bomb. Government broadcasting can be a public service or a barrage of disinformation.

The push for the Strategic Defense Initiative (SDI) has opened up a global dialogue on the uses of space. One possibility, under discussion in Europe, Canada, and the U.S., is an international satellite monitoring agency (ISMA), through which all countries would have the right to high-resolution observation of Earth from space. An ISMA could be established by treaty, through the U.N., or on a regional basis. The main sticking point would be access to military information, and whether the policy would really be "open skies."

The concept of space as "common property" (established by the U.N. Outer Space Treaty in 1967) could be taken further, however, to its fullest expression—a World Forum. The idea is that each country should get "air time" to broadcast to the rest of the world, using satellites along the GSO. Much of the broadcasting would probably be cultural, but some countries would use their time every month or two for news or propaganda. A Forum, even with the limitations imposed by repressive states and unequal budgets, would help to break down myths, barriers, and misconceptions.

Establishing and operating a World Forum would take an

estimated half a billion dollars a year (less than half a percent of the world's annual spending on arms) and would require a corps of 1,100 translators. If it could be established, it would surely reduce the dominance of superpowers over world affairs. Nicaragua and Burundi would have the same time on the air as the United States or China. Their ideas might well be more consonant with permanent world peace than the clashing ideologies and military alliances of the blocs. In any case, we could all consider their ideas independently of military firepower—an exciting and hopeful prospect.

Mary Cotton:

ONE THOUSAND LOCAL STATE DEPARTMENTS?

Michael Shuman has a dream—a dream of an "international union" of local officials dedicated to reversing the arms race and resolving conflicts. Michael Shuman, through his organization, the Center for Innovative Diplomacy (CID), has begun laying the groundwork for bringing his dream into being.

"National leaders have been uniformly unresponsive to citizen demands for disarmament," he says. "What's needed are new strategies that give citizens the opportunity to build their *own* foreign policies."

What will keep CID from becoming just another public policy institute?

"A number of things," says Shuman confidently. "To begin with, we are not focused on Washington. We believe that local governments are potentially the most powerful actors in international affairs right now. We also believe that if you can't do it in your own backyard, it can't be done or shouldn't be done (anywhere).

"Second, we are focused on acting and doing, not just writing and thinking. In our canvassing, in our workshops, in our consulting with elected officials, we are presenting and, in a way, testing what we are writing about."

CID's strategy for building municipal foreign policies focuses equally on national, local, and international levels.

National: CID is working closely with Local Elected Officials of America (LEO), an organization dedicated to "rechanneling" military spending back to America's cities. LEO was organized by Larry Horan, a city councilman from ultraconservative Irvine, California. Larry and Michael do workshops together on how local officials can create plausible foreign policies at the municipal level. "We are *not* advocating isolationism. If anything, we're encouraging a new kind of interventionism, and we're encouraging local governments to have hearings on human rights policies abroad . . ."

Local: Shuman continues "to suggest just how far local governments should go in influencing foreign affairs. We are developing a proposal for a Global Affairs Council within the Palo Alto city government. It would have jurisdiction in all foreign affairs and national defense issues. (It could do) education, research, lobbying and litigation.

"Its three to five members would be elected in the same manner as city council people. This would encourage candidates to run for office and debate different foreign policy viewpoints.

"It would have the authority to spend 1 percent of the city's budget . . . if other cities would follow Palo Alto's example . . . the current level of money available for grassroots peace work could be expanded enormously."

International: In August of 1985, in Hiroshima and Nagasaki, two hundred local officials in thirty countries came together for the World Conference of Mayors for Peace through Inter-City Solidarity. Through CID's behind-the-scenes lobbying efforts, the mayors of Hiroshima and Nagasaki committed themselves to holding a second expanded conference.

Shuman's long-term plan transcends present day politics: He hopes CID will develop hundreds, perhaps thousands of municipal state departments around the world. "Representatives from each would be involved in (an) international body (which) . . . would have more legitimacy than any assembly of national governments—because a local government is closer to the people . . .

"By transforming rigid nation-against-nation conflicts into fluid alliances of cities, where cities will ally on some issues and disagree on others, there is a better chance of creating more complex global politics where no one disagreement can lead to war between large geographic blocs of nation-states . . ."

Peter Jarman:

DÉTENTE FROM BELOW

You can't get away from it. The Bolsheviks seized power in Petrograd (Leningrad) in October 1917; Communist parties seized power in Central and Eastern Europe in the late 1940s. Europe's divided. *They* drive society differently on the other side of the divide. They're different. But who are they? Friends or partners?

To heal this divide, people need to meet. People-to-people over kitchen sinks can disarm their anxieties, their fears, their enemy imaging, their megamegatons of weapon capability, and their mutually assured destruction. But who are the 'they'? Friends or partners?

Someone proposed recently that we should refer to people like us (independent autonomous peace groups) in the East as friends, and to the Party people in official peace councils as partners. Friends have the same bloodstream of loving relationships, of upholding individual rights and social justice. Friends speak the same language. Partners are different. They share responsibility for the survival of the planet Earth, the one Europe, our common enterprises. Partners have to adjust and to accommodate their differences. Not by complete trust as friends, that would be too great a risk, but as discerning partners with a necessary but probably limited trust in each other. They have common ground, but deep differences.

The Quaker approach is to seek that of God in every person; to be faithful to a love that listens and affirms the divine spark within all. Since our beginnings in the English revolution we have listened to people in power and have spoken the truth to them as we have perceived it. (Our) truth about the human condition. We therefore seek out first the people in power in socialist states. And they, with their knowledge—in principle if not in detail—seek the company and challenge of those that are not in power, recognizing that all people are indispensable elements of a civil society.

Let's be more adventurous in making friends and knowing our partners in the East. Young people especially. Seize every chance, including invitations from Communist youth organizations, being aware of their traditional drills (the large scale organizing of 'world youth festivals,' for example). Use such meetings to make contacts in corridors, on streets and in flats.

And listen to what public and private voices say, often several voices in one person, and seek to understand your discussion partners so that you could give an account of their views they would recognize as authentic.

On first meeting a young Soviet academic and party official four years ago, we warmed to each other. I said that if he would give me the American reasons why détente came to an end I would give him the Soviet reasons. "If we can give each other more than eight marks out of ten for acceptability," I said, "we'll carry on talking. Otherwise we must do our homework first." We let each other pass that test. Four years later, we are still in touch. We met last Easter by the kitchen sink of his flat by the Neva River—for an eight hour chat about Springtime in Soviet affairs. That released a lot of tension. That is what détente from below is about.

Dietrich Fischer:

NONINTERVENTION

The United States, the Soviet Union, France, and in earlier times a host of other European countries have repeatedly felt the urge, even the duty, to intervene militarily abroad to "set things straight." These interventions have sometimes achieved their objectives to bring to power a "friendly" government, at least temporarily, and have sometimes failed. So far they have not yet led to a direct confrontation between the superpowers, more by luck than design. But that possibility, which might escalate into a nuclear war, cannot be excluded forever.

Let us consider one of the United States' latest interventions, the invasion of Grenada, which was popular with much of the United States public. Over some years, the Reagan Administration had prepared the public by raising the specter of a Soviet military base in the Western Hemisphere (the airport being built on Grenada at Salinas). When the opportunity to intervene arose in Grenada, Reagan seized it and installed a pro-U.S. government. In that process, Soviet diplomats were rudely searched and expelled, and a number of Cuban construction workers were killed. We are lucky that the Soviet Union exercised restraint and did not intervene to protect its citizens.

Imagine if the reverse had happened. The United States has indeed built military bases in the Eastern Hemisphere—for example on Crete and on the Island of Diego Garcie in the Indian Ocean—not just civilian airports. Suppose one morning 6,000 Soviet paratroopers had landed to drive out the American construction workers and install a pro-Soviet government. It is doubtful that the United States would have sat by idly. It would probably have sent several carrier task forces to retake the island. If the Soviet Union had reacted this way in Grenada, it could have been the beginning of World War III. Of course, there will always be violent events in small countries around the world, like the coup in Grenada, but this does not mean that it is the United States' or anyone else's task to intervene. If we see it as our task to "restore order" in such cases, we in effect hand over the decision whether our country is at war or peace to small dictators and would-be dictators around the world. This is like connecting a powder keg to dozens of fuses, any one of which may be ignited at any moment. This is not a "security policy," but an almost perfect insecurity policy.

Dietrich Fischer:

A HUMAN "PEACE SHIELD"

President Reagan called the Strategic Defense Initiative (SDI, or Star Wars) a "peace shield." At the same time Defense Secretary Weinberger stated that if the Soviet Union developed such a system before the United States, it would pose a grave threat, since the Soviet Union could then attack the United States without fear of retaliation. Of course, the same applies in reverse, which explains the Soviet Union's concern about space weapons.

Proceeding with SDI would therefore lead to a vast new round in the arms race. It could also precipitate the outbreak of war during a crisis. Space stations would be extremely vulnerable. If war appeared imminent, each side would feel under great pressure to destroy the space weapons of the other side before the other side could destroy its own. SDI could also raise the specter of accidental war, since the time to react is so short that it would not allow for human intervention. A faulty computer program could start World War III. The solution to the problem of nuclear weapons does not lie in a technical fix. It is basically a political problem, and must be addressed as such.

The improvement in U.S.-Chinese relations shows how rapidly the threat of nuclear war can be overcome, if there is interest on both sides. In 1969, during the big debate whether the U.S. should build an anti-ballistic missile (ABM) system, the argument was made that it was not yet feasible to build a "dense" ABM system against Soviet missiles, but that was not so important. The Soviet leaders were relatively reasonable and reliable. The great danger was the Chinese, they were so fanatic and unpredictable. All the U.S. really needed was a "thin" ABM system to keep out Chinese nuclear missiles. Today the U.S. is not afraid of a Chinese nuclear attack, but not because of any thin ABM system. It is because of our improved relations with China. Twenty-seven thousand Chinese students are in the United States, and a quarter million U.S. citizens visit China each year. There is growing trade between our two nations. Both sides have a high stake in maintaining those good relations, and neither side is thinking remotely of launching a nuclear attack on the other side, which would also be an attack on its own citizens. This has reduced the mutual fear of a nuclear attack. A greater exchange of people is like a "human peace shield" that helps prevent war.

John K. Stoner:

A CONFLICT MANAGEMENT MODEL FOR WORLD PEACE

his is a time of hope. People are rediscovering the
importance of simple, elementary things. Pure water.
Clean air. Safe streets. The right to live.

In such a time we may discover that the foundations for a
peaceful society are simple, if not easy. A society needs truth,
justice, diligence, and discipline. The foundation most lacking
for a peaceful world may be the last of these—*discipline.*

A peaceful society, whether defined in as small a unit as
Pennsylvania or as large a unit as the United States, accepts the
discipline of acting in accordance with rules. These rules define
the boundaries of acceptable behavior in inter-personal relationships. There may be—indeed, there certainly is—a great
deal of disagreement and even conflict within a peaceful society.
But the rules for managing that conflict are understood and
accepted. A society which is at peace observes, pervasively and
overwhelmingly, the discipline of nonviolence.

The discipline of nonviolence is, essentially, the rule that
people will not kill one another. It may not be an easy rule to
observe, but no civilized society takes that as a reason to
abandon the rule against killing.

A conflict management model for moving toward world
peace accepts the fact that there will be a conflict between
peoples and nations. It is therefore not a utopian model. A
conflict management vision sets limits. It requires only that all
of life's inevitable struggles shall be dealt with in some decent

172   GLOBAL

way, without resort to such methodologies as slavery, torture, terrorism, or war.

Why is the practice of killing people in war so vigorously defended, and even deemed honorable? War, like robbery, murder, and rape, may be inevitable, but that is not a reason to think it honorable.

But, because it is thought acceptable to kill people on an international scale, we have what we have in the arms race, a national budget wildly out of control over military spending, a federal deficit which ruptures every brain that tries to imagine it, and the tragic prospect of global nuclear suicide. All of this because we reject the discipline of a simple rule—People should not kill people.

At this point the question arises: "Could this simple rule be implemented in practice?" Two things urge an affirmative answer. First, it already has been almost universally implemented. Over five billion people observe it in interpersonal relationships on a daily basis. That is a high level of observance for any rule. Second, the discipline of a rule that people should not kill people does not have to be easy in order to be right.

Why do those who defend the necessity of war so glibly assume that the first requirement of any alternative is that it must be easy? Why should nonviolence be easy? Why should it not require training on a scale as grand as the vast educational establishment of the armed forces? Why should it not require funding on a scale just as vast?

Nonviolence has not been tried and found wanting. It has been found difficult and left untried. This is not good enough for the potential of human society and the reach of the human spirit. God has something better in mind.

Let us accept the discipline of a conflict-management model for the human family. Let us set some boundaries for our behavior, agree not to kill each other, and live with the consequences. A basic commitment to the discipline of nonviolence is the foundation of every peaceful society. This truth, which admits of no exceptions guarantees that the discipline of nonviolence is the foundation for world peace as well.

John Marks and Jim Garrison:

U.S./USSR: AN OPPORTUNITY FOR A GENUINE CONTRIBUTION TO GLOBAL WELL-BEING

For reasons of both self-interest and humanitarian concern, the U.S. and USSR have a stake in the problems of the Third World being solved, or at least, not getting out of control. Otherwise, superpower security is threatened as the planet becomes increasingly precarious.

We suggest that the two superpowers could isolate areas of mutual concern and work jointly to deal with pressing problems that are, in truth, shared by all. At first, such collaboration would have to be *in addition to,* not *instead of*—continued conflict in such places as Afghanistan, Nicaragua, and Angola.

By cooperating, the superpowers would be taking positive steps toward improving relations; making a genuine contribution to global well-being; and developing a new, constructive model for interaction in the Third World—a model that might someday supplant the current one.

We have suggested this idea to numerous Soviets and Americans—with encouraging responses. We found a consensus in both capitals to avoid trouble spots and set up small, do-able projects in countries like India or Tanzania where the superpowers enjoy relatively good relations. Such efforts should leave a legacy of personal and professional relationships; they should involve Soviets and Americans in fields where both can make a significant contribution; and the host country should be included as an equal partner.

Possible areas of cooperation include:

174

● HEALTH: A joint medical team could staff a Third World clinic or fight an epidemic. In the past, U.S. and Soviet doctors worked together in the global effort to wipe out smallpox. There is now collaboration to meet the World Health Oranization's goal of immunizing the world's children against killer diseases.

● ENVIRONMENT: A mixed group could help clean up a chemical spill or prevent desertification. Ecological awareness is a key part of Gorbachev's "new thinking," particularly since Chernobyl and the success scored last year by Soviet environmentalists is blocking government plans to reverse the flow of Siberian rivers.

● ENERGY: U.S. and Soviet experts already cooperate in developing new and more efficient energy sources. They could expand this cooperation to applications for the developing world.

● EMERGENCY AND DISASTER RELIEF: Soviet and American teams could provide emergency supplies and medical relief after earthquakes, floods, and other natural disasters.

● SATELLITE MONITORING: Both superpowers could use their non-military satellite surveillance systems to provide Third World nations with weather data and natural resources analyses.

● BOOK EXHIBITS: Private and governmental groups in the U.S. and USSR regularly sponsor foreign book exhibits and author tours. Joint exhibits, organized on such subjects as health promotion and environmental protection, would help bring badly needed expertise to the Third World.

Beyond the deadlocked "mega-issues" that separate the U.S. and USSR, the two nations could act to find solutions to Third World problems. Their enlightened self-interest makes for a realizable area of Soviet-American common ground—an area that cries out for action now.

Gene Knudsen Hoffman:

JOINT VENTURES WITH THE USSR

The Soviets threaten us because they're afraid of us. And we threaten them for the same reason. "The threat," according to Robert Fuller, former president of Oberlin College, now peacemaker-at-large, "isn't that they're hoping to conquer our land—they couldn't govern it if they had it—nor we theirs. The greatest threat is our fear of each other."

I've been searching for new, creative ways of approaching the Soviet people directly in what Fuller calls "Track Two Diplomacy." To do this we must be people who specialize in introducing different cultures to each other. We must describe our values and lifestyles *without discounting* those of the Soviets, and we must invite them to do the same.

To make peace we must search for common ground, and then work together from that. Here are some ways I believe we can do it.

The Soviets suffer severe food shortages. We often have a surplus. We could assure them that we will sell them wheat at a fair price into the indefinite future. We will not allow their people to go hungry.

The Soviets have a high alcoholism rate and they acknowledge this. So do we. Alcoholics Anonymous is already in the Soviet Union, teaching the Soviets about AA. Among its basic tenets are that members must relinquish blame, fear, resentment, and self-pity—then they must forgive all who harmed them. Anyone following this program can have no enemies.

Both our nations have housing problems. Both have working mothers. Both need new and innovative ideas on shelter and

176   GLOBAL

child care. These are areas where we can share our skill and "know-how" to the benefit of both of us.

Both nations have land areas subject to "perma-frost"—an area so cold the ground never thaws out: Alaska and Siberia.

Both are seeking ways to make these areas liveable. Surely we could meet and discuss our common problems and share what each has learned.

—There are more teachers of English in the Soviet Union than there are students of Russian in the United States. Studying and teaching Russian is an initiative for peace.

—Nish Jamgotch of the University of North Carolina describes fields in which the United States has benefited substantially by cooperation with the Soviets: basic physics, laser treatment of glaucoma, studies of air pollution, light-weight concrete construction technology, the effects of long-term space flight on cosmonauts.

Our working together has created small areas of trust, leading to the relaxation of international tensions. There are ancient philosophical and spiritual reasons for proceeding toward peace this way, on personal, grass-roots levels.

For example, there is a Buddhist practice—"If you feel anger and aggression against someone, give that person a gift." One cannot continue to feel anger and aggression while thinking about giving a gift. What a turn-around it would be if we thought of the gifts we might give someone we fear. We might begin with "win-win." Some of us believe there can be no successful peace conference unless both sides receive equal benefits, both experience a "win."

Robert Muller:

VISIONS OF OUR NEEDS

In Memory of Paul G. Hoffman,
Administrator of the Marshall Plan and of
the United Nations Development Program.

On this vast and vital subject, I would like to make the following comments and proposals:

1. We need a major and resounding international report on violence in the world and on remedies and alternatives to it. We need to highlight the facts, statistics, trends, forms, and varieties of violence and *attempts at solutions around the world in all fields*: from child-abuse, street violence, crime, land occupation, high-jacking, and terrorism to violence between nations. Such a report should be followed by a world conference against violence and/or an International Year against Violence.

2. While our primary concern, especially in the West, is with physical violence, we should attach no less importance to verbal violence, to violence in communications and the media, and to the origin of all violence: violence in the mind. The Eastern philosophies can make a great contribution in this respect. They teach that the mind can contain only one idea— if it is a negative one, replace it with a peaceful one, and the negative, violent ideas will disappear. This should be taught to children and practiced up to the heads of states.

3. There should be more interest and support of the United Nations and of its agencies, which are the first worldwide organized efforts to fight against war and violence in all its

forms: the causes of violence (hunger, injustice, etc.) and to replace them by cooperation and positive action.

The U.N. is probably the greatest world repository of alternatives to violence, but as Paul Hoffman used to say: "It is carefully hidden from the public"—perhaps by advocates and beneficiaries of the status quo. Most of the information required for the report on violence is available from the U.N., but does not reach the public. The objectives of a report by eminent world personalities would be precisely to bring that information to the public.

4. As long as heads of states give the example of violence—physically through wars and armaments, mentally through violent thoughts and speeches, sentimentally through hatred and denigration, and through a lack of spirituality—how can people be expected to be peaceful, kind, loving, and nonviolent?

The example of nonviolence, peace and cooperation must therefore come from leaders of nations. Perhaps a new International Year of Cooperation is needed to lay the foundations of the next millennium as the Millenium of World Cooperation.

5. We need a completely new vision and ideology of peace and nonviolence on this planet at this stage of our evolution. The vocal, but outdated ideologies born in the nineteenth century—capitalism and communism—must be transcended into an ideology of proper care and management of our unique planetary home. All the building blocks for such a new vision have been assembled in the U.N., but are by and large ignored.

6. We need a spiritual revolution on this planet, the upgrading and validation of individual human life, the recognition that each individual human being is a precious, sacred entity of divine, heavenly, or cosmic origin, meant during a short life of consciousness to fulfill a meaningful function. No human being should be left without meaning, without a contribution to the human ascent toward a peaceful, fulfilled, Godly human society on this planet.

All people in all professions, especially all leaders, should ask themselves what their cosmic responsibilities and meanings are. Above all, the leaders of the U.S. and of the USSR must ask themselves that question.

7. If you want peace, teach peace. If you want alternatives to violence, teach alternatives to violence. A revolution is needed in education. I would recommend that educators from all over the world take an interest in two first manifestations of that revolution: an elementary school in Arlington which teaches children to live in right relationships with their human family and with their planetary home—and to play their intended optimum role in the unfolding of time on this planet. The second is the University of Peace recently established by the U.N. General Assembly in Costa Rica. In that university, peace and nonviolence will be made a total science, as war and armaments were a total science heretofore. Strategies, methods, meetings and training for peace will be organized on every conceivable face of the vast canvas of human life, from the individual and the family to the total family of nations. The young peacemakers and leaders of tomorrow will be trained and will meet each other on the campus of that first supra-national university. It will give people a tremendous opportunity to take the world in their own hands.

8. The time has come when each individual should take the matters of this planet in his or her own hands, associate with like-minded people within nations and across nations; vocally and financially support individuals, organizations, and international associations working for peace, nonviolence, and a better world. Each human on this planet should belong to such a group.

Fran Peavey and Charlie Varon:

WEAPONS ANONYMOUS

FRAN AND CHARLIE ARE IN DIFFERENT PLACES IN THE AUDIENCE

FRAN: (*stands up to testify*)
It feels really good to be with people who have the same problem I have. It's kind of hard to talk about. Thank heaven this group is anonymous.

You know, when I got started, I didn't think it would lead to this. But before I knew it, it had become the most important thing in my life. I'd wake up in the middle of the night, just terrified and shaking. I don't have to tell you how awful it is— you've all been there, right? I didn't THINK I was addicted, until one day, I needed a cruise missile before breakfast.

Then I started taking money from the poor to pay for my habit. I noticed I was lying to my friends and family. I started to be afraid all the time—afraid that people would notice my addiction and call me on it, and try to get me to change. And I started HIDING MY MISSILES: first I buried them and then I put them under water, then I tried to put them up in the air. (*Gets excited:*) And then I had this idea that I could just move them around, I was REALLY EXCITED about that, because then I could have a missile wherever I wanted one, and nobody could find them to take them away from me! I tell you, these weapons became an obsession!

CHARLIE (*stands up*)
I know just what you mean! (*Walks over to Fran*) Like the test launches: I mean, they DO something to me!

There's a physiological reaction. When they tested the cruise missile up in Canada—boy, talk about excitement! All that power and strength! Oh wow—it was WONDERFUL!

FRAN

I can identify with what you say, but you know—I don't get off on it anymore. (*Moves closer to Charlie*)

CHARLIE

Don't get so close to me.

FRAN

(*Moment of truth, quietly:*) Don't you feel—sometimes at night, when it's dark and you can't sleep—don't you kind of hit the truth that it's time to stop?

CHARLIE

Hey look, I don't NEED nuclear weapons. (*Dances a little:*) See, YOU may be addicted, but I can handle my missiles. I could stop any time I wanted to. I could disarm tomorrow if I wanted to. I don't NEED nuclear missiles. (*Sheepishly:*) I just like the feeling they give me. Don't I deserve that? Hey look, we're adults, we can handle this. We're not children. It's perfectly natural. It's been going on for a long time. I's a part of being human.

FRAN

But this issue is larger than just you or me. Look how you're paying for your habit. You're stealing the children's lunch money, and there have BEEN accidents. This is not just an addiction—we have a *disease*. We're SICK! And you're sick with a sickness you don't even know you have. It's time to disarm now!

CHARLIE

Well, aren't YOU being self-righteous? If you really feel a need to disarm, if you can't handle your missiles, give them to me. I can take care of them. Wouldn't I have disarmed 20 years ago if I could have? If I disarmed now, I don't know if my system would survive the shock. Look around you. We're in a real world, and these weapons have kept us out of a world war for forty years, they may have saved millions of lives.

Do you want people to start talking behind my back, saying, 'He's weak now. NOW we can take advantage of him.' Do you WANT to be speaking Russian? If I give up missiles, how am I going to feel strong? You tell me how can I get that same sense of power, that same sense of security, that same sense of destiny. What would you have me do instead? Meditate?

FRAN (*Defenseless:*)
You know, it took me a long time to admit that I was addicted, that I was powerless over my addiction, and that it was killing me. I feel like I'm fighting for my life—and my children's life, and their unborn children. What about YOUR children?

CHARLIE
I don't want you all to think I'm being unreasonable. I've often said I'd be willing to sit down and talk about disarmament. But you have to try to see it from my point of view. It's very frightening to think about giving up these weapons. I feel boxed in. It's terrifying to go on and it's terrifying to stop.

Blackout—

Frank Kelly:

A DAY OF CELEBRATION
FOR HUMANITY

Each year, perhaps on the anniversary of the UN's founding, perhaps on New Year's Day, there should be a worldwide celebration of humanity's greatness—emphasizing the creative manifestations of the previous year in all nations.

For twenty-four hours, beginning at dawn and ending on the next dawn, the beauty and the wonder of human beings should be presented in films broadcast around the earth.

Dancers, singers, musicians, poets, artists of all kinds—from all nations—should display their abilities. So-called ordinary people should be given opportunities to tell about moments of joy they have experienced. Pictures of persons whose eyesight has been restored by modern surgery— the eyes of people who see the delightful colors and shapes around them with fresh sight—should be shown to the world, to remind every human being of the marvelous gift of *seeing*. While these films are being shown, glorious music should be played. The words of prophets and seers from many places, speaking many languages, should be heard. The cries of mothers giving birth, the voices of children babbling at play, the voices of older people speaking of what life has taught them, should also be broadcast.

Violence usually arises from a lack of self-esteem. Millions of people do not appreciate their own worth. The purpose of this celebration should be to shout to the universe that human beings reflect the deepest mysteries of that universe. Scientists might speak of how we are made of the same stuff as the stars— that we draw our strength and our creative potency from the fiery energy with which the universe was endowed from the beginning.

"The extravagant gesture is the very stuff of creation," Annie Dillard declared in *Pilgrim at Tinker Creek*. "The whole show has been on fire from the word go!"

The day of celebration would be free of violence. The day would remind every human being of all the mountains that have been climbed, all the peaks that have been reached. It might end with the singing of the *Ode to Joy* which concludes Beethoven's Ninth Symphony—with the choir drawn from every nation.

Such a day could give us new ways of *seeing*, as well as a surge of hope. With hope, we can see the ways out of our terrible dilemmas. With hope, we can pass through the agony and attain the ecstasy beckoning to us.

Robert Muller:

DECIDE TO NETWORK

Decide to network
Use every letter you write
Every conversation you have
Every meeting you attend
To express your fundamental beliefs and dreams
Affirm to others the vision of the world you want
Network through action
Network through love
Network through the spirit
You are the center of a network
You are the center of the world
You are a free, immensely powerful source
Of life and goodness
Affirm it
Spread it
Radiate it
Think day and night about it
And you will see a miracle happen:
the greatness of your own life.
In a world of big powers, media, and monopolies
But of four and a half billion individuals
Networking is the new freedom,
the new democracy
a new form of happiness.

Contributors:

Joseph Abileah lives in Israel. He is the architect of the Middle East Confederation as a solution for that beleaguered land. He is a lifelong pacifist.

Louis Perez Aguirre is founder of SERPAJ (Service for Peace and Justice), a nonviolent group in Uruguay. He is a Jesuit priest who studied in Canada, France, and Spain. He works with the poor of his country.

David H. Albert is a father, writer, and veena player. He is founder and editor at New Society Publishers (Santa Cruz, California), the nation's only publishing house dedicated to social change through nonviolent action.

Clifton Anderson is a professor at the University of Idaho; Citizen Diplomacy is a vital interest. He helped create the Borah Symposium, a Moscow, Idaho, to Moscow, USSR, Channel for Peace.

Andrea Ayvazian is director of training at the Peace Development Fund in Amherst, Massachusetts, and is a member of Mt. Toby Friends Meeting.

Albert Baez is a U.S. citizen born in Puebla, Mexico. He is volunteer president of Vivamos Mejor/USA, an organization dedicated to bringing science to communities in Mexico and Central and South America.

Ronald Beasley lives in Scotland. He is a long-time peace activist and is the former president of the International Fellowship of Reconciliation.

Wendell Berry's writings are dedicated to the renewal of ourselves and the earth through the cherishing of people and places.

Donna Bradley and her husband are Quakers who have created a

Very Special Home for Very Special Children. Her work is to adopt and care for children who have been severely abused.

A.G. CHIKANDAMINA was born and lives in Zimbabwe. He is the Christian and African representative to the International Fellowship of Reconciliation.

MARY E. CLARK teaches biology at San Diego State University, where she teaches a course called "Our Global Future." She won an award for her part in helping San Diego step forward—toward peace.

FLORIA COON-TEETERS is presently co-chair of International School Psychologists Committee on Conflict Resolution and Disarmament.

MARY COTTON is a pseudonym for an activist author.

RICHARD DEATS is Disarmament and Peace Secretary for the American Fellowship of Reconciliation. His work covers the U.S.A., the USSR, South Africa, and the Philippines. He taught nonviolence to Protestants for the recent revolution.

DANIEL DEUDNEY is a fellow of the New World Policy Institute, co-author of *Renewable Energy,* and the pamphlet *Whole Earth Security.*

ALAN R. DRENGSON is associate professor of philosophy at the University of Victoria in Canada. He is a writer and editor and holds a black belt in Aikido.

GENIE (EUGENIE) DURLAND is a mother of five, a war-tax resistance counselor, a teacher of peace studies and feminism, a dreamer of dreams, and a believer in the future.

JUDY ELLISON was at one time executive director of the Clearinghouse on the Future of the U.S. Congress.

PAT FARREN co-parents Jesse, Caitlin, and Gabriel, and edits *Peacework,* a New England peace newsletter of the American Friends Service Committee. He has one book: *What Will It Take to Prevent a Nuclear War?*

DIETRICH FISCHER is associate professor of computer science at Pace University. He is a visiting fellow at the Center of International

Studies at Princeton University. His book is *Preventing War in the Nuclear Age.*

RICHARD WENDELL FOGG, PH.D., directs the Center for the Study of Conflict and is developing the concept of nonmilitary defense in event of nuclear threat or limited attack.

JAMES FOREST is executive secretary of the International Fellowship of Reconciliation in Holland. His new focus is a media project for IFOR and his most recent book (in progress) is on the Russian Orthodox church today.

DIANA FRANCES is a Quaker with a pacifist and church background. She is president of the International Fellowship of Reconciliation. Her main interest is to help restore a sense of self-respect and potential to young people.

MAURICE FRIEDMAN is a professor at San Diego State University. He was a conscientious objector during World War II. He is spiritual kin to all Quakers and a prodigious writer. Among his books are three on Martin Buber's life and work.

ROBERT FULLER is former president of Oberlin and a physicist by education. He is co-founder and participant in the Mo-Tzu movement, a loosely connected group who travel the earth seeking new visions of peace and practicing citizen diplomacy.

CLAUDETTE GAGNON is housewife, mother, and grandmother. She graduated with a B.A. in music, teaches piano, takes care of her husband, who is starting a Pax Christi group while she does her best in the adult choir.

JIM GARRISON is author of *The Russian Threat,* and is executive director of the Esalen Institute's Soviet-American exchange program in San Francisco.

CHELLIS GLENDINNING is a psychologist who co-founded the international peace network Interhelp. She is the author of *Waking Up in the Nuclear Age.*

KEN AND GERALDINE GRUNOW are obviously good and thoughtful people; however, their essay arrived so close to press time that we could not include biographical information.

GREG GUMA has been a writer, editor, and organizer since the sixties. He edits *Toward Freedom,* a magazine on non-alignment, and owns and operates the Maverick Bookstore in Burlington, Vermont.

AMOS GVIRTZ was born in Israel and lives on a kibbutz, is a pacifist and a vegetarian, and formed the first chapter of the International Fellowship of Reconciliation in Israel to help Israelis and Palestinians resolve their differences nonviolently.

JULIET HILLS is a children's librarian; born in England, she values wildlife, land, and flexible education in the U.S. She longs for English villages, feeling small communities offer more opportunity for commitment and accountability.

DAVID HOFFMAN is a founder of Interhelp and the Mo Tzu School of Citizen Diplomacy. He is director of the Congressbridge Project and co-director of Internews. He was national director of Survival Summer, and editor of *Evolutionary Blues.*

ERIK THORKILD HOFFMAN was a conscientious objector in the Vietnam War. He is past president of the Santa Barbara Co-op and is now office coordinator for the radio series "The Other Americas"; he plays the guitar and sings.

ROBERT HULL is Secretary for Peace and Justice for the Mennonite General Conference. He has been editor of *God and Caesar,* a quarterly newsletter on military tax concerns and is chairperson of the National Campaign for a Peace Tax Fund.

DEENA HURWITZ is on the staff of the Resource Center for Nonviolence in Santa Cruz, California. She is co-chair of the Middle East Task Force of the New Jewish Agenda and serves on the AFSC Northern California Mideast Subcommittee.

PETER JARMAN is the East-West Secretary of Quaker Peace and Service in London, England. His focus is on U.S.-USSR relations.

MARY EVELYN JEGEN is a sister of Notre Dame, a penetrating thinker, a devout woman. She is vice president of Pax Christi USA, formerly chair of the National Council of the FOR and was arrested for praying at the Pentagon.

FRANK KELLY espouses "found causes" in Santa Barbara (the homeless, adult education), is senior vice president of the Nuclear

Age Peace Foundation; he has written a history of the Center for the Study of Democratic Institutions, of which he was once vice president.

GENE KEYES left Harvard in 1961 to join the Committee for Nonviolent Action, burned his draft card in 1963, and served a prison term of eighteen months. His focus has been nonviolent defense by the military. His contribution is excerpted from his book, *Force Without Firepower*. He is a birthright Quaker.

GENE KNUDSEN-HOFFMAN is the mother of seven (adult) children, and a Quaker; she has pursued careers in theater psychology, writing, and peace. Today she pursues reconciliation—bringing together those who have been set apart—hence this book.

FRANCES KENDALL is a young white South African, an outspoken opponent of apartheid and an outspoken *pro*ponent of cultural, ethnic, political and economic diversity. She co-published a best-seller: *South Africa the Solution*.

YEHEZKEL LANDAU was born in the U.S. and lives in Israel. He is a graduate of Harvard Divinity School and is now information director of Oz ve Shalom, an organization of religious Zionists for peace.

LEON LOUW is a young white South African seeking alternatives to apartheid.

JOANNE MACY is co-founder of Interhelp; a charismatic speaker, she is author of *Despair and Personal Power in the Nuclear Age,* and of the source book for her contribution, *Dharma and Development.*

JOHN MARKS is executive director of Search for Common Ground, an organization devoted to developing common ground between the U.S. and the USSR.

CAROL MOORE is with the Libertarian, Green, bio-regional, decentralist and war-tax resistance movements. She's editor of *Decentralize,* a quarterly newsletter. Her contribution, excerpted here, was first published in *Peace Conversion Times.*

DON MOSELEY is on the National Council of the FOR, a founder of Jubilee Partners, a long-time center for the integration of races and for refugee relocation. His work is now mostly with Central America.

MARKLEY MORRIS is former editor of *WIN* magazine.

ROBERT MULLER is former Assistant Secretary General to the United Nations, former president of the University for Peace in Costa Rica, and is the author of many books and poems, including *Best of All They Taught Me Happiness*.

PHIL McMANUS is Latin American staffperson for the Resource Center for Nonviolence, on the Steering Committee of Witness for Peace. He is co-editing a book on Nonviolent Action in Latin America.

MICHAEL NAGLER is obviously a good and thoughtful person; however, we have no biographical information.

PEACE PILGRIM was a woman who gave up her home, her private life, and her personal identity to become a wandering pilgrim for peace. After walking over 25,000 miles, she was killed in an automobile accident.

FRAN PEAVEY AND CHARLIE VARON are two peace activists and social change people who created the Atomic Comics. They give their messages in more conventional ways as well—like books, and Fran's commitment to de-polluting the Ganges.

MARY PORTER CHASE has taught pre-school, elementary, junior high, and college levels. With her life-partner, Shirley "Sam" Masser, she writes, practices Buddhism with her Taoism, and care-takes the land in Sonoma County, California.

ANN MARIE QUINLAN IHM is retired in Florida and is chair of the new Diocese for Venice Peace and Justice Commission, which emphasizes eliminating the death penalty.

FRANCES SALANT received a Quaker education, raised a family, and became a mental health worker. She now leads experiential workshops in prisons for the Alternatives to Violence Program of the New York yearly Meeting of Friends.

MARK SATIN is the editor of *New Options*. He recognizes and honors all green, fresh, and fertile thought. He is author of *New*

Age Politics, his first attempt to capture the emerging new analysis, strategy, economics, ethics, and worldview.

MARK SHEPARD is a freelance writer, and a Quaker; he lives in Arcata, California. His five-month visit among India's Gandhians is described in his new book *Gandhi Today,* the story of the Mahatma Gandhi's successors.

DOROTHY SAMUEL, Quaker, author of *Safe Passage on City Streets,* believes peace people have no right to protest actions between governments unless they demonstrate ways of peace. Her areas of expertise are personal violence and women's issues.

JONATHAN SISSON, at 43, is General Secretary of German-speaking Swiss FOR, has studied comparative religions, classical philosophy, and theology at Kenyon College and the University of Basel (Switzerland).

MASHA SOLOVEYSCHIK, who lives in the USSR, attended an Interhelp workshop given in the USSR, was invited to contribute to *Ways Out* by a friend. She did. Mila Tosherova Shaw graciously translated her essay.

TOBY STEFFIAN is a pseudonym for a freelance writer who masks his identity when his daughter's privacy is involved.

JOHN K. STONER is an executive secretary of the Mennonite Central Committee; born in 1942 and raised on a farm, he celebrates God's goodness by spending time out of doors. He and his wife Janet have five children.

JOHN VASCONCELLOS is assemblyman from the 23rd District in Sacramento. He believes the best of his opponents and asks for their help. His hero is Carl Rogers and he practices unconditional regard for everyone.

KURT VONNEGUT, JR., is the author of the remarkable book *Cat's Cradle* and many others. His contribution is from a speech he gave in New York City in 1984. It was first published in *The Nation* and subsequently in *Fellowship Magazine* in 1987.

HAROLD WILLENS is an industrialist who wakened to our nation's advance into militarism during the Vietnam War. He founded

Businessmen Against the Vietnam War, and co-founded the Center for Defense Information in Washington, D.C.

CAROL S. WOLMAN-CLAPSADDLE is married and has two children; a practicing psychiatrist, active in her local Jewish and Christian communities, she was a founder of Interhelp and first president of the Bay Area Physicians for Social Responsibility.